Tactical Leadership

The Compass Great Leaders Use To
Stay On Course

STAR Performance
Uniting Planning and Doing for a High-Performance Leadership Model

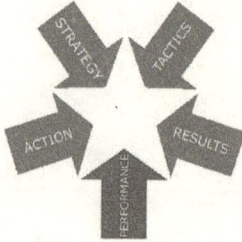

Discover the fundamental relationship between strategy, tactics, action, and results. Learn to unify each of these critically important aspects of performance to achieve STAR Performance.

Strategic Leadership
Discover Your Map | Empower Your Future

Discover your map for leadership. Your journey begins with a review of organizational leadership theory and builds through to the development of the STAR Leadership™ model. Learn to apply the Seven Postulates and the Four P's of Strategic Leadership that define your map, and empower your future.

Centurion Living
Life Planning Fundamentals

Learn the real meaning of life, and how to live with purpose and mission. Change your perspective on life and gain a whole new passion for living.

Tactical Leadership

The Compass Great Leaders Use To
Stay On Course

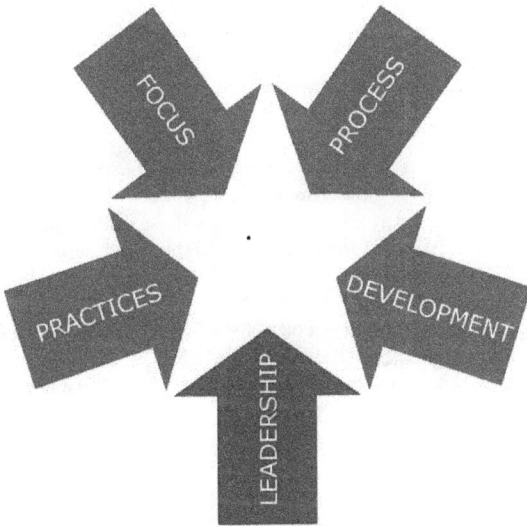

Justin Thompson, PhD

2Xalt Press books may be ordered through booksellers or by contacting:

2Xalt Press
An Imprint of 2Xalt, Inc.
Viera, FL 32955
www.2Xalt.com
+1.321.430.4258

Excellent discounts on quantity orders for bulk purchases or special sales are available from 2Xalt Press. Order a box today for use in training programs, NPO fundraisers, corporate gifts, book sales, and other events. Visit Press.2Xalt.com for more information or call us at the number above.

2Xalt Press provides a range of authors and subject matter experts for speaking events. To learn more, visit 2Xalt.com or call +1.321.430.4258.

Because of the dynamic nature of the Internet, any web addresses or links contained in this book may have changed since publication and may no longer be valid. The views expressed in this work are solely those of the author and do not necessarily reflect the views of the publisher, and the publisher hereby disclaims any responsibility for them.

Unless otherwise noted, Scripture quotations are from the ESV® Bible (The Holy Bible, English Standard Version®), copyright © 2001 by Crossway, a publishing ministry of Good News Publishers. Used by permission. All rights reserved.

ISBN: 978-0-9978157-2-6 (sc)
ISBN: 978-0-9978157-3-3 (e)

Printed in the United States of America.

2Xalt Press rev. date: Feb 2018

Contents

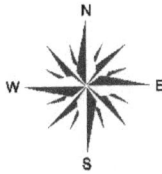

Introduction

In *Tactical Leadership*, we're going to look closely at how to put the concepts of STAR Leadership™ into action. This will include an analysis of where our leadership **focus** should be, the **processes** of leadership that will guide us in behaving like STAR Leaders™, key **practices** that STAR Leaders™ must adopt for everyday use, and the ongoing leadership **development** that is essential to sustaining STAR Leadership™.

FOCUS

PROCESSES

PRACTICES

DEVELOPMENT

As with the concepts in *Strategic Leadership*, the applications through leadership focus, leadership processes, leadership practices, and leadership development are extensions, revisions, and improvements upon the prior work of generations of thought leaders. Nearly 900 years ago, John of Salisbury, an English scholar, and bishop, quoted Bernard de Chartres, an 11th century French philosopher and professor of logic and grammar, as stating that the achievements and ideas of his time were of value because their developers were "perched on the shoulders of giants", and "that we see more and farther than our predecessors, not because we have keener vision or greater height, but because we are lifted up and borne aloft on their gigantic stature."[1]

The same is true for the concepts presented in the STAR Leadership Trilogy. *Strategic Leadership* builds on the evolution of organizational leadership theory, and *Tactical Leadership* stands on the shoulders of the giants of applied leadership. The concepts and ideas of multiple "giants" in leadership theory and their applications serve as the foundation for STAR Leadership™, which combines the best of prior ideas and expounds upon them to produce new approaches and improvements to how we lead and influence others. In time, others will improve upon the ideas presented here. Perhaps you will learn from these ideas and develop them further to improve upon them yourself.

How to Use this Text

This text is designed as a study in the practical applications of leadership. It is meant to help you improve your understanding of what it means to be a leader, and ultimately to improve your leadership skills. *Tactical Leadership* is the

---

[1] Salisbury, John of. *Metalogicon*. Trans. Daniel D. McGarry. Berkley: University of California Press, 1955. Web. 28 July 2016. <books.google.com>.

second book in the STAR Leadership Trilogy (*Strategic Leadership*, *Tactical Leadership*, and *Performance Leadership*).

While each volume in the trilogy can stand alone on its own merit, you will reap the most benefits when you view, understand, and apply the 'big picture' of STAR Leadership™.

I have left a wide margin on the outside edge of each text page within the book. The intent is to provide space for you to take notes and write down ideas that come to you as you read. Occasionally, I have placed a note in this margin space to highlight important points that I believe will be helpful for you to remember.

Enjoy your journey into the application of STAR Leadership™ as you explore the principles of *Tactical Leadership*.

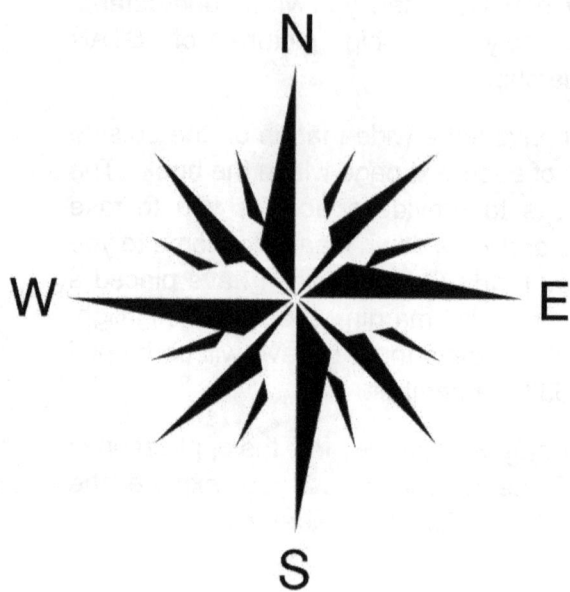

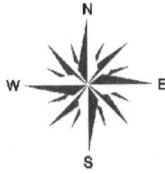

Map and Compass

For the leader, strategy is the map by which one locates their current position, identifies the desired destination, and plots the course between the two. With a good map, this vision of the desired destination can be carefully planned. In *Strategic Leadership* I presented an overview of leadership theory and how it has evolved over time – eventually reaching what I call "STAR Leadership™". STAR Leadership™ is high-performance leadership built on the principles sound strategic leadership, utilizing powerful tactical leadership tools, and achieving high-performance results.

Having the best map in the world isn't enough. In my youth, I enjoyed an activity called orienteering in which my friends and I would carefully review a topographical map that showed terrain features, trails, roads, boundaries, water, and more. We would search the topographical information for hints of something interesting – a remote waterfall or pool, or a bluff with an interesting view. We would intentionally find spots that didn't have road or trail access, so we were crossing remote wilderness in Western North Carolina to get to the desired location. When you are out in the wilderness, a map is essential, but a map alone won't do you much good.

We would each carry a copy of the map in a sealed plastic bag to protect it from rain, and a special compass similar the one in the image. We knew that having the map alone would only show us our starting point and our destination, but without the compass, we would lose our bearings and become totally lost during the journey.

To identify our location, we would seek out three unique landmarks. They had to be unique enough to be able to visually locate them and identify them on the map. The compass would be used to measure the angle at which you were viewing the landmark, and then draw a line at that angle on the map, passing through the landmark. We then knew that we were somewhere on that line, but we had no idea how far we were from the landmark.

After repeating the process with a second landmark, we'd have two lines on our map. If our measurements and drawings were perfect, we'd be exactly at the intersection of these two lines. This would tell us precisely where we were on the map, and we could update our path to the intended destination. Unfortunately, this process is never exact. For this reason, we would always look for a third landmark.

Again, if measurements were perfect, the three lines would intersect at the same point. They never did. Instead, we'd have a small triangle on the map, and we'd know that our current location was somewhere in that triangle. Usually, the triangle was very small so that our location was accurate enough to plot our new course. Occasionally, we'd need to look for even more landmarks to make the area identifying our likely location smaller and more precise.

This is exactly how we want to approach leadership. A leader is influencing others to get from point A (where you are) to point B (the desired destination). If the leader can't identify the location of these points accurately, how will he influence others to join him on the journey? No one wants to follow someone into the wilderness to get completely lost.

Strategic Leadership – leadership built on the "strong roots found in a firmly defined purpose, unshakable principles, and forward thinking demonstrated through passion inspiring vision and persistent effort" – provides the essential map.[2] *Tactical Leadership* is the compass providing you the ability to identify your location at any point in

---

[2] Thompson, Justin. *Strategic Leadership*. 2Xalt Press, 2016. 111

your journey, key 'landmarks' along the way, and potential obstacles or items of interest that may exist across your path.

The strategic leadership tool – a "map" that indicates your core leadership theory and core leadership ideology – gives you the big picture perspective on your journey. The tactical tools – your "compass" built on sound leadership focus, an effective leadership process, and empowering leadership practices – is the only way to reliably follow the map.

Remember that leadership map is built on a core leadership theory and expressed in a core leadership ideology – this is *Strategic Leadership*.[1] The full description is provided in the book, *Strategic Leadership*, and the brief outline provided below will help jog your memory and put you in the right frame of reference for getting the most from *Tactical Leadership*

Strategic Leadership

Core Leadership Theory

There are seven postulates defining great leadership. The first, the Foundation Postulate, defines and communicates Purpose, Principles, and Passion; and demonstrating Persistence. The second, the Service Postulate, indicates that STAR Leaders™ are called to serve. The Focus Postulate is that STAR Leaders™ focus on both results and relationships. The Function Postulate reveals that leadership is a function of behavior. The Alignment

Postulate states that there must be alignment between purpose and vision, between organizational structure and strategy, and, lastly, between operations and strategy. The Adaptability Postulate teaches us that our style of leadership, our leadership behaviors, must adapt in response to the experience and expertise of those that we lead, as well as the priority level of the task, and the risk tolerance. Finally, the Coaching Postulate reminds us that STAR Leaders™ practice E^3 Coaching™ - Encouraging, Empowering, and Enabling.

Core Leadership Ideology

The Core Leadership Ideology is the foundational definition of a worthy cause, rock solid values, inspiring vision, and consistent devotion. In STAR Leadership™, this is expressed as the *Four P's of STAR Leadership™*: Purpose, Principles, Passion, and Persistence – as defined in the Foundation Postulate.

Strategic Leadership is forward-looking. Unfortunately, the concepts are often less popular and their importance overlooked because the positive impact takes time to materialize. You apply the concepts immediately, but the results pay off in the future. The impact of *Tactical Leadership*, however, is immediate. It will be felt as soon as the concepts are implemented. While *Tactical Leadership* provides an immediate impact, its value is greatly limited without the long-term vision of *Strategic Leadership*. To be a STAR Leader™, you must implement both *Strategic Leadership* and *Tactical Leadership*!

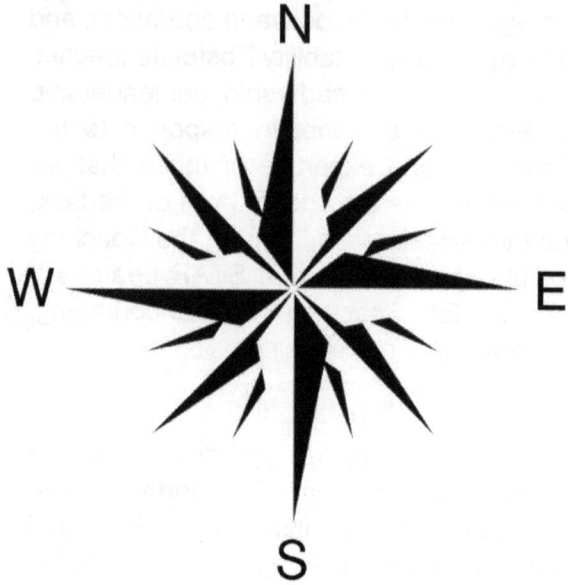

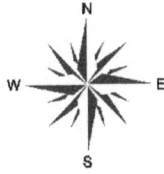

Leadership Focus

Omnidirectional Leadership

How will you focus your leadership efforts? STAR Leaders™ know that leading is not just about guiding those who are subordinate to them on the org chart. In fact, great leadership requires a focus of leadership efforts in all directions. I call this concept *omnidirectional leadership* because it is a three-dimensional focus in every possible direction.

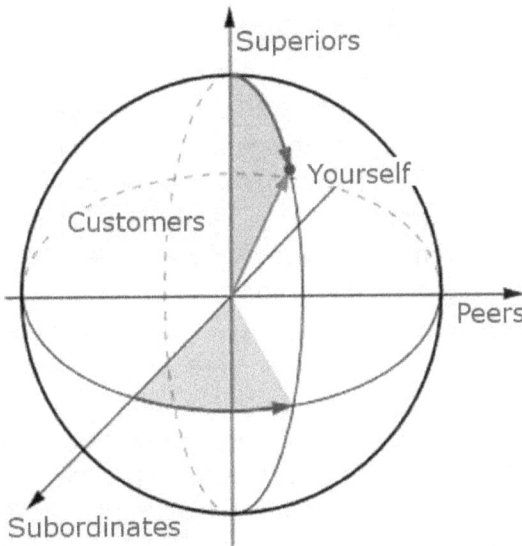

Figure 1
Spherical Coordinates Illustrate Omnidirectional Potential

This means a leader has the potential, if not the responsibility, to lead those around him – not just those subordinate to him in the organizational hierarchy. Great leaders will lead everyone that they serve. This means leading your subordinates, leading your peers, leading your superiors, leading your friends, leading your family. As a matter of fact, STAR Leaders™ never stop leading, regardless of the setting and regardless of the audience.

Remember that *leading* does not mean giving orders. There are times when *giving orders* may be a practice of leadership, but leadership is ultimately about influence. You can influence anyone if you have a heart that desires to add value to who they are or what they are doing.

> You can influence anyone if you have a heart that desires to add value to who they are or what they are doing.

Bill Hybels notes that "In the heat of battle, the *leader* must be in the center of the action. It is the leader who must feel the pressure first, hear the sounds first, smell the smells first, and sense the momentum of the way things are going long before anyone else. *Every soldier deserves such competent command.*"[3] There are two key takeaways from this message. First, the leader must be in the center of the action. When you are at the center of something, there is a sphere of influence around you. That is, there are people, projects, organizations, customers, goals, objectives, etc.; you have the potential to influence any or all of them. Secondly, leaders take the heat first. They aren't just pushing their teams into action, they are setting examples and expecting their teams to follow their lead.

According to leadership author and teacher John Maxwell, "The reality is that 99-percent of all

---

[3] Hybels, Bill. (2008) *Leadership Axioms*. Grand Rapids: Zondervan. 161-162

leadership occurs not from the top, but from the middle of an organization."[4]   Think about this statement for a moment! He is implying that only one percent of organizational leadership occurs in the C-suite. The majority of leadership – influence that guides progress – occurs within the ranks of the organization. This showcases the importance of *omnidirectional leadership* and the ability that leaders have, to influence others in all directions.

Most importantly, before we can lead in any direction, we must also first change our own perspectives as well as the perspectives of others about who and what leaders really are. The most popular misconception about leadership, according to Maxwell, is "the belief that leadership comes simply from having a position or title."[5] Leadership isn't a position or title. It's a calling that is open to anyone and everyone.   Leadership can be expressed in all directions on the organizational chart hierarchy.

Leading Subordinates

Leading subordinates is probably the most obvious direction of leadership focus. It is what is built into or heavily implied through job descriptions, compensation and incentive plans, operational procedures, and organizational charts.   To be effective at leading organizational subordinates you must develop and communicate purpose and vision. You must clarify expectations and hold everyone accountable, treat every individual with the utmost of respect, be discerning and decisive, empower your team to succeed, and be both kind and firm.

Principles for Leading Subordinates

Clarity

Empowerment

Corrective Actions

Humility & Respect

Loyalty

---

[4]   Maxwell, John C. *The 360° Leader*. Nashville: Nelson, 2011. 1.
[5]   Ibid. 4.

Clarity

Leaders must provide clarity for their followers. Every team member requires clearly defined roles and responsibilities, as well as clear expectations. There should be no doubt about organizational objectives, team goals, or the goals of individual team members. Everyone should know what the core purpose of the organization is, what the non-negotiable principles are, and what every element of the vision is.

As the leader, you must frequently talk about purpose, principles, and vision. It's up to you to make these core elements a part of everyday conversation.

As the leader, you must frequently talk about purpose, principles, and vision. It's up to you to make these core elements a part of everyday conversation. In addition, leaders need to personally communicate with the individuals on the team to ensure that they understand their own goals and are consistently making progress towards those goals. Don't allow the excuse that, "I needed X and you never provided it." Make sure you know that X (whatever X might be) is needed and that you give ample opportunity for individuals to make their needs known early in the process. Go get X – meet those needs so that your team can excel, and the goals will be met.

Empowerment

Ken Blanchard teaches that "empowerment means letting your people bring their brains to work and allowing them to use their knowledge, experience, and motivation to create a healthy triple bottom line."[6] This is an important concept. Literally speaking, the word *empower* refers to the transferal or delegation of power or authority to another. When you empower someone, you give them the power do something themselves – you authorize them to take matters into their own hands!

Note that empowerment is not synonymous with entitlement. Entitlement is being given something or being guaranteed the receipt of something. It is the assumption or assertion that because of X, you are entitled to Y. An entitlement may, or may not, be something that you have earned, but it generally does not come with any expectations of responsibility. For instance, social security is an entitlement that is earned. You spend a working lifetime paying into the program, setting aside monies for your retirement years. After a certain age or the onset of disabilities that removes you from the wage-earning workforce, you are entitled to receive a return on that investment. There are no further expectations placed on the recipient of social security payments.

Empowerment is the delegation of power and authority, and it comes with an expectation of responsibility.

Empowerment is the delegation of power and authority, and it comes with an expectation of responsibility. Throughout my years of experience in leadership roles, I've had the responsibility of mentoring and coaching many professionals. One of these responsibilities involved determining salary increases for those that reported to me. At the end

---

[6]   Randolf, Alan and Ken Blanchard. (2007) "Empowerment is the Key." In Blanchard, Ken. *Leading at a Higher Level.* (67-86) Upper Saddle River: Prentice Hall. 67.

of each fiscal year, a few subordinates would demand a pay increase greater than the amount offered. My response would always be one simple question – "Why?" Their responses always revealed much about what I, and the organization for which we worked, could expect from them in the coming year. Some would arrogantly respond with a statement such as, "I've been with this company for X number of years, so I believe I'm entitled to this raise." To which I would always reply, "This organization is not in the business of entitlements. If you want that kind of raise, you've got to show how you're going to add that kind of value to the bottom line, so the company can afford to pay you that much more."

Others would tell me how their certifications or advanced degrees they had earned in the past year made them more marketable. In other words, they would have to be paid more if we wanted to keep them on the team. I don't like threats, so my response to such demands would generally be something like, "It's been nice having you on our team. I hope your new employer receives the value that your demands imply. Can I help you pack your desk?"

I don't mean to sound callous, but I believe strongly in rewarding individuals and teams for jobs well done, and just as strongly in not offering a reward when the job is not done well.

Now, when an employee responded to my question of "Why?" with a well-thought-out explanation of the value that they have contributed, and how they will continue to contribute in the future, then I would eagerly review the financial value of that contribution and how much of a raise we could afford to give them, and then give the raise. I would also make it clear that the raise is an empowerment, not an entitlement. In other words, I now had certain expectations and would be reviewing those expectations with them on an ongoing basis.

Although I have done "annual reviews" of my subordinates in the past, I don't like the concept. These types of assessments tend to pile up 365 days' worth of feedback into one single discussion. Instead, I think feedback and performance reviews should have more of a coaching feel. The head coach of a football team doesn't wait until the end of the season to tell team members what they are doing well and what they need to improve. He provides this feedback the moment they walk off the field! When we are leading subordinates, we need to do the same. Correct failing behaviors immediately, and reward success on the spot. Sometimes those rewards are monetary, and sometimes they are a pat on the back or a compliment, such as "Great Job!"

My point is simple. Avoid a culture of entitlement and cultivate a culture of empowerment. Give appropriate levels of decision-making authority to people and let them know the responsibility that comes along with that empowerment. Now, there's an old saying: "If you want something done right, you'll have to do it yourself." This is one of the most foolish and short-sighted sayings of all time! I'd say that if you want people to improve over time, so they do things right even when you're not looking, mentor and train them. That's how improvement is cultivated.

If you want people to improve over time, so they do things right even when you're not looking, mentor and train them.

When you do everything yourself, you create a bottleneck. If, on the other hand, you empower others, you will become a force multiplier that adds ten- or even one hundred-fold the value to the organization that you serve!

Corrective Action

Servant leadership is a significant part of being a STAR Leader™. Being a servant leader means serving the cause first, but it also means serving the individual. Empowerment is the best way to serve individuals and increase the value of force multiplication in the process. Corrective action is also a powerful way to serve those that you lead. Sometimes leaders will become soft because they think serving their team means never confronting them. These leaders are confused.

When mistakes are made, corrective action is required for others to learn and grow from those mistakes. When poor behavior is evident, corrective action is required to put the behavior back on track and help the individual be the best contributor to team success that they possibly can be. Colin Powell once said, "If a follower knows that he has just made a mistake and gotten away with it, he loses confidence in the competence of the leader and has less respect for him."[7] Corrective action should be decisive and immediate. The ability to carry out such corrective action in an effective, fair, and encouraging manner is the responsibility of the STAR Leader™. Even more importantly, Mr. Powell noted that "Leaders who do not have the guts to immediately correct minor errors or shortcomings cannot be counted on to have the guts to deal with the big things."[8]

---

[7] Powell, Colin and Tony Koltz. *It Worked for Me in Life and Leadership.* NY: HarperCollins, 2012. 91.
[8] Powell. 92.

When making these corrective actions, do so in a meek manner. Read that carefully – I said meek, not weak. Weak means without power, authority, or intention. Meek means showing care and kindness when giving corrective action while still being firm and steadfast. If you have children, think about parenting for a moment. A weak parent loses complete control of the child. A child picks up on this weakness at a very early age. We've all seen unruly children in the grocery store, grabbing things from the shelves, screaming relentlessly, or throwing a temper tantrum until their parents give in to what they want.

On the opposite side of the spectrum, an overbearing parent maintains control but breaks the child's spirit in the process. Even if being overbearing doesn't involve violence, as far as I'm concerned, I would consider this to be child abuse. A child's spirit should be tempered but never broken, disciplined but never destroyed. Rather, the meek parent can calm the child with a look, or a soft-spoken comment. Of course, no parent is perfect. This is just a simple reminder that poor behavior has undesirable consequences, and good behavior is rewarded. Every child will act out and push boundaries to test them. Meek parents steadfastly maintain boundaries yet do so in a manner that reassures the child of their love rather than doubting it.

This is exactly how the STAR Leaders™ need to act with their subordinates, by providing meek leadership that is humble, caring, flexible where appropriate, yet steadfastly fixed on maintaining the boundaries that matter.

Let me give you an example from my own experience. I recall sitting in an office conference room giving a presentation to a potential client when I happened to look down the hall. I noticed the peculiar sight of a baby squirrel playfully walking down the hallway headed straight for our meeting room! I remained writing on the dry erase board and simply closed the door to the conference room, carrying on with the meeting.

Later that morning, after completing the meeting with my prospective client, I began inquiring about this mysterious squirrel. It didn't take long for me to discover that one of our employees had "adopted" three baby squirrels whose mother had apparently been killed at a nearby construction site. I also learned she was keeping the squirrels in a basket in her office, and that several people had found "droppings" on their desks, and even on the table in the breakroom! Apparently, everyone that knew about it was afraid to report it because this employee was the child of the owner, who happened to be my boss!

Obviously, I had to put an end to this immediately. I went to her office and let her know that while I appreciated her care and concern for wildlife, the office was not a suitable home for the squirrels because it would teach them to be depended on people, and they would no longer be able to survive on their own in the wild. And, not only did the squirrels create a safety concern for every employee, they also had the potential of wreaking havoc should they sneak into a meeting with clients! I gently let her know that we would be implementing strict pest control practices the next morning and that it would be best for her squirrels if she found a more appropriate home for them before then.

My next stop was a visit with our facilities person, asking him to place some rodent traps around the office. Then I visited with my boss, the employee's father. He, of course, had already heard about the plan by the time I got to him. I assured him that we had the problem under control. Within 24 hours there would be no more rodents, including squirrels, in the office. I also told him that his daughter had been encouraged to find a more appropriate home and that they would not be harmed in the process. I sensed that he might be prepared to tear into me in defense of his daughter, but instead, he laughed at how I handled it and said, "Carry on." The squirrel adopter took a little bit of extra time for lunch that day, but she took the squirrels with her. During my entire interaction with her, I never yelled at her, only speaking with a firm but gentle tone. And, I never saw those squirrels again!

To bring things full circle, let me quote Mr. Powell once again: "Kindness connects you with other human beings in a bond of mutual respect. If you care for your followers and show them kindness, they will reciprocate and care for you. They will not let you down or let you fail. They will accomplish whatever you have put in front of them."[9] To clarify further, he said, "Being kind doesn't mean being soft or a wuss. Kindness is not a sign of weakness. It is a sign of confidence."[10] That's meekness – humble, kind, confident, and steadfast leadership.

Humility & Respect

This demonstration of meekness and kindness segues into respect. We often think that followers should demonstrate respect for their leaders in the workplace and not vice versa. However, respect is

---

[9] Powell. 23.
[10] Powell .48.

omnidirectional. It is also about leaders respecting the value of someone's contribution. Yes, it is important for us to respect the authority and expertise of those we follow. But, it is equally as important for us, as leaders, to value everyone in the organization. I've always believed that it is important for a leader to be humble and demonstrate that no task is beneath them.

When I was President of a small company of about 25 employees, we had a housekeeper that came once a week to clean. During the week, trash cans became filled to their rims, and bathrooms got dirty. I made a point of letting everyone in the company know that it was their responsibility to keep things clean, rather than allow trash to pile up and bathrooms to get disgusting between the housekeeping staff's weekly service visits. Now, to mentor and develop this culture, I didn't look for someone to tell to clean the bathrooms or take out the trash. I was usually one of the first people in the office each morning, and I often scrubbed toilets and emptied trash cans before others arrived. Most of the employees most likely never witnessed me doing those chores, yet word got out that I was willing to do everything that I asked others on the team to do. I always took great pride in my team! After a while, when I checked the bathrooms and the trash cans in the mornings, I often found that someone had already taken care of them the evening before.

Respect is both a willingness to do the very tasks you expect your followers to do and proactively expressing value in people at every level.

Respect is both a willingness to do the very tasks you expect your followers to do and proactively expressing value in people at every level. The housekeeper that I mentioned above is just as valuable and worthy of respect as any assembly technician, engineer, salesperson, accountant, manager, president, or board member. Each have different roles, but they all serve the same purpose and are contributing to the success of the same vision. If the housekeeping never got done, the office would be a wreck and it would be impossible to complete any of the technical work. I may have had different conversations with the Chairman than I had with the housekeeper because they have different interests, concerns, and roles, yet I showed them both the same amount of respect.

Loyalty

Loyalty to your people is part of showing them respect. When you value someone, you are loyal to them. In every leadership position I've held everyone that reported to me knew that in private I would hold them accountable and would confront any mistake or behavior problems head-on. They also knew that in public I always had their back. For instance, when I was leading a team of product developers, one of the engineers made a careless mistake that was going to set us back several weeks. This engineer was a highly talented product developer that was generally very reliable. He simply slipped up and made an honest, but careless mistake.

In a design review, my boss was leaning on this engineer rather toughly, and pushing me to do the same. Instead, I interrupted my boss every time the conversation got unpleasant for the engineer in question. I politely made it clear that the responsibility for the delay was squarely on my shoulders, and my shoulders alone. Not only that, but the responsibility for recovery was also on my shoulders! It was important for me to let my boss know that I would do everything in my power to expedite the recovery process, and it was equally important for me to let the entire product development team see firsthand that I would never throw any of them under the bus. They needed to know that I was more interested in how they handled the recovery than in making a big deal out of the mistake that was made. The truth is, I also needed them to be free to make mistakes because, without mistakes, success tends to be hard to find.

Later that day, I had a private conversation with the engineer that made the mistake. I was firm, but also kind. I asked him to do two things: First, I wanted a recovery plan on my desk before the end of the day, and second, I wanted an analysis report detailing the lessons learned from the mistake and any procedural changes we might make to reduce the risk of recurrence. Towards the end of the day – well after the traditional 5 p.m. "whistle" – I stuck my head in the product development lab and witnessed the entire team rallying around the engineer, helping develop the recovery plan. Not one of them had been asked to help, but many of them had witnessed me taking responsibility for the delay during the design review.

Over the next couple of weeks, that team worked 16+ hour days, even though I never asked them to do so. What we estimated as a three- to four-week delay ended up being about a week and one-half! We still made the final product release date on time. In addition, the team made procedural changes during the recovery process that made the likelihood of repeating the same mistake very small. I never did receive a written analysis report, because, after a couple of informal conversations with the team, it was clear what had been learned. The resultant changes were already in place, so I told them the verbal analysis report was sufficient.

Loyalty is about standing by your team. It's about establishing an expectation that you'll have their back when they need it.

Loyalty is about standing by your team. It's about establishing an expectation that you'll have their back when they need it. The funny thing about loyalty is that when you are loyal to followers, they tend to be equally as loyal to you. Rudy Giuliani observed that "[Ronald] Reagan would risk his popularity because of his personal loyalty to people who had stood by him, helped elect him, and worked for him. You cannot believe what that did to boost the morale of his organization."[11]

It's important to point out that care must be taken not to be loyal to a fault. Loyalty must be a two-way interaction, and when a follower is taking advantage of your loyalty to get away with inappropriate behavior, poor performance, or outright dishonest gains, you must take decisive action. I'll share several examples that will clarify what I mean.

The first example is that of a young engineer hired to be on a team that I led. He had multiple degrees, looked good on paper (for a rookie), and interviewed well. After getting him on the team and assigning tasks to him, it became evident that he didn't possess the baseline knowledge and skill that his degrees had implied. I brought him into my office to privately discuss my concerns, worked together with him to develop an improvement plan, and promised to review progress with him again in 30 days. I also provided clear expectations as to what needed to be accomplished and demonstrated

---

[11] Giuliani, Rudolph W. (2002). *Leadership*. NY: Miramax. 235.

during that 30-day period, and the consequences that would result from failing to meet those expectations. He tried; he really did. Unfortunately, he just didn't have it in him to be an engineer in that environment.

At the completion of the 30-day period, I asked him to come to my office to talk. I began by emphasizing the strengths that I saw in him, and then explained how he had failed to meet the expectations. The consequences were removal from the team – I had to fire him. This was tough because he was a good kid that really tried hard. But he just didn't have the skills or knowledge that were needed to perform the job.

He was heartbroken at being fired from his first job, but the team was relieved because he apparently had slowed progress on every project he "helped" with. It was the right thing to do. Even though my actions didn't appear to demonstrate loyalty to the individual, they definitely demonstrated loyalty to the team. As it turns out, his termination was the best thing that happened to him. I followed his career for a few years after that and noticed that he found work he was much more suited to do. I'm sure that his new position brought him much more fulfillment than working in an environment that he wasn't properly prepared for.

A second example comes from my observations of a very dishonest and self-centered colleague. This individual hid inventory to keep it off the books so that his monthly numbers looked better. He intentionally sabotaged projects in other departments to keep them from interfering with his own agenda, or to distract attention from his mistakes. He was two-faced in how he dealt with people – telling you one thing to your face and doing something entirely different behind your back. He was extremely talented – the problem was that he often utilized his talents in very dishonest ways. Everyone that worked with him knew this about him, and no one trusted him. He should have been terminated. Instead, his supervisor took the wrong approach to loyalty, and had him relocated to another division where his impact would be "out of sight, out of mind." The dishonest behavior didn't go away, it simply found new outlets, and placed the responsibility for the dishonest behavior in another supervisor's lap.

Ultimately, this bad seed made great gains for himself within the organization by conning and manipulating his way up the ladder until he became the general manager of the very division that should have terminated him in the first place. Sadly, the result was low morale, high turnover, slumping performance, abandonment of the vision, and the eventual closure of the division.

One final example – I had been leading a small team of technicians responsible for keeping an entire manufacturing plant running smoothly. I had known about the pending closure of the plant for a few months but didn't learn about the official announcement until a few days before it was to happen. The plant was being sold to a competitor and would close in three months. All the equipment would be relocated to the new owner's facility and staffed by their people.

Right before the announcement was to be made, I was scheduled to depart for Europe that Tuesday. I would be overseas when my team would learn that they were going to be laid off. Originally, I was supposed to spend a couple of days with the customer and do some sightseeing in Normandy before returning home. I left on Tuesday as planned, landed in Paris, and drove late into the night to be at the customer's facility in Normandy on Wednesday. After meeting with the customer during the day and solving their problems, I drove all night Wednesday night to get back to the airport in time for a Thursday flight. I arrived back in the U.S. very early Friday morning and went straight to the office so I could be there when the announcement was made.

I pulled my maintenance techs aside to reassure them. I let them know that I had known about the closure for a couple of months, and had already been working behind the scenes to assist them. The company owned all the tools that these techs used, but regionally, maintenance techs were often required to have their own tools. This meant finding a new job would be much easier if they had their own set of tools. I convinced the corporate office to consider the techs' mobile workstations as part of the incentive package to keep them in place until they were no longer needed. In other words, if the techs stayed on the job until we closed the plant, they could keep their tools and workstations. This was several thousand dollars' in value, and more importantly, it would make them much more marketable to other companies.

Over the months that followed, I made it my mission to help the techs find new jobs. I made phone calls and visits to other manufacturing plants. I reviewed their résumés and conducted mock interviews with them. They knew that I cared about them and was loyal to them. As a result, they not only stayed on the job until the end, but they also created several process improvements before turning the equipment over to the new owner. And, by the time we closed the plant, these techs had jobs elsewhere.

Leading Peers

Successful peer leadership grows from the heart of a servant leader. Servant leaders always work at helping others and adding value to their efforts. To do this, you must be both perceptive about what people need, and proactive in meeting those needs. It has been said that "Leading colleagues rests upon two principles: understanding need and delivering value."[12] I would add to this a third principle: building trust. If your peers don't trust you, they won't allow you to see their needs and will prohibit you from providing value. Ken Blanchard said, "At its best, leadership is a partnership that involves mutual trust between two people who work together to achieve common goals."[13]

Principles for Leading Peers

Recognizing Need

Delivering Value

Building Trust

There are three distinct attitudes that you as a leader can choose to have about your peers: competition, indifference, or that of a teammate. When you are competing with your peers, you will naturally find it challenging to help them in their efforts. You will not be motivated to add value to their performance. In fact, you'll be tempted to behave in such a way as to remove their value, or at least hide it. When you are indifferent to their success, adding value to their performance will not be high on your priority list. In fact, it may not be something that you think about at all. When you truly think of your peers as teammates, you go out of your way to help them and add value. You want to make them look good because that makes the team look good.

---

[12] Baldoni, John. "When Leading Peers, Value is Power." *Forbes.* 18 Mar 2015. Web. 22 Mar 2016.
[13] Finch, Fred and Ken Blanchard. (2007). "Partnering for Performance." In Blanchard, Ken. *Leading at a Higher Level.* (117-144). Upper Saddle River: Prentice Hall. 117.

Consider professional football, for example. During the preseason, when team performance is irrelevant, players are competing for their spot on the team. The business world equivalent to that example would be the interviewing and candidate selection process. At that point, you are competing with every other applicant. You need to emphasize the value you bring to the team. But, once the regular season starts, you want everyone on the team to be dedicated to the performance of the team. If the quarterback is competing with the wide receiver, you've got problems. When the quarterback has the wide receiver's best interest in mind, the two are going to connect in high-performance ways.

In business, if the production and engineering department heads are competing with one another, the performance of the company is going to suffer. The two departments aren't going to work efficiently together, and office politics will become the norm. But, when the department heads have a mindset of teamwork, engineering will make production more efficient and production will provide quality feedback to engineering on design adjustments that could make the product better or lower manufacturing costs. Each department will perform better, and the organization will reap the benefits.

Therefore, peer leadership, in effect, servant leadership across the organizational chart, is essential to maximizing organizational performance. And when you are known for adding value to the efforts of your peers, you will become significantly more valuable to the organization. John Maxwell states, "Competent leaders can lead followers. They can find, gather, recruit, and enlist them. This is no easy task, but a leader who can lead only followers is limited. To make it to the next level of leadership, a leader must be able to lead other leaders – not just those below them, but also those above and alongside them."[14]

Leading Superiors

Leading those above you on the organizational hierarchy can be tricky. Yet doing so is essential to organizational success, your superior's success, and your own career growth success. To lead your organizational superiors, you'll need to be bold and take initiative, add value, prepare relentlessly, build trusting relationships and stay loyal to the mission.

Bold Initiative

Having bold initiative requires a self-starting nature without fear of risk. Speaking frankly and truthfully with superiors can be difficult and risky. Not all leaders welcome the truth. But, great leaders are always open to hearing it. In fact, more than being open to it, they will demand it. Leaders that punish the bearers of bad news end up having no one to tell them the truth when things go awry. When supervisors such as these create an environment of fear, they end up getting blindsided because no one speaks freely. The truth is, "Sometimes those above you just don't yet see what must be done, and your calling is to spark their attention and move them along a course of change before it is too late."[15]

To break that pattern, you'll need to be a bold leader that is willing to risk suffering the consequences of sharing bad news. Bad news should be shared with those it impacts as quickly as possible. To soften the blow, I always recommend bringing a potential solution, or at least a plan for taking steps towards a solution, whenever possible.

Principles
for
Leading
Superiors:

Bold
Initiative

Add Value

Prepare
Relentlessly

Build
Relationships

Loyalty to
the Mission

---

[14] Maxwell. *The 360° Leader*. 159.
[15] Useem, Michael. (2001). *Leading Up*. NY: Three Rivers. 4.

Add Value

Always having an attitude of adding value to the team, to the organization, and to your superiors makes taking the bold initiative easier. That's the idea behind providing a solution when reporting a problem. John Maxwell states that leading superiors can be the leader's biggest challenge, but "If you take the approach of wanting to add value to those above you, you have the best chance of influencing them."[16] Michael Useem, a professor at the Wharton School, teaches that "leadership is a matter of bringing more to the office than we were given, of adding greater value to the company or country than it would have achieved without us."[17] In other words, STAR Leadership™ is a matter of giving more than you take and providing more value than you receive.

STAR Leadership™ is a matter of giving more than you take and providing more value than you receive.

One part of adding value is being honest – even when honesty hurts. As stated previously, there will be times when you must be the bearer of bad news. There will be times when you must critique your leader's ideas, and there will be times when you must push back on the direction your leader is taking. It's important to know that there are times when you need to speak up, and there are times when it's best to remain silent. When something is critical to the success of the organization or the mission, you need to speak up. When something is of a more personal nature and not as critical to the organization or the mission, don't push as hard.

---

[16]   Maxwell. *The 360° Leader*. 81.
[17]   Useem. 2.

How do you add value to your superiors? Demonstrate a willingness to do whatever it takes to make them successful. Be willing to perform tasks that others are hesitant to take on so that you become the "go-to-guy" (or "go-to-gal") that your boss relies on. In short, each of the other principles of upward leadership will help you add value. Bold initiative makes you the one that can be counted on. They know you won't sugar-coat the message or add fluff, but that you will tell it like it is, whether good or bad. Furthermore, relentless preparation will put you in a state of perpetual readiness for whatever comes along. Building relationships allows you to know people and helps you bring the right people together to solve problems. Loyalty to the mission makes you passionate about the success of the team.

Prepare Relentlessly

Relentless preparation means that you are constantly striving to learn new things and that you are forever seeking out the information that will put your boss in a positive light. It also means that when you have a meeting planned with your supervisors, you are thoroughly prepared so that you can deliver the message efficiently and avoid wasting any of their time. John Maxwell teaches, "You show your value when you show that you value your leader's time."[18] If you approach a meeting with your leaders in an unprepared manner, you are wasting their time. Don't be the one that wastes their time. Instead, be the one that is prepared and efficient.

Always being prepared also makes it possible to remain calm in the face of significant challenge. Life, as well as business, is oftentimes challenging. If you're always ready for a challenge, it won't knock

---

[18] Maxwell. *The 360° Leader.* 127.

you off your feet. In fact, preparation is the key to turning a challenge into an opportunity. You know the old saying, "When life hands you lemons, make some lemonade." To successfully do this, you've got to be prepared for it. If you have a juicer and a pitcher handy, you'll be ready to make lemonade when life hands you some lemons.

If you have a juicer and a pitcher handy, you'll be ready to make lemonade when life hands you some lemons.

Part of preparation is also knowing what your superior wants to hear. For example, if your superior is concerned about production yield, and you prepare a thorough report on employee morale, you may not be providing what is really needed. It might be good information, but is it the right information at the right time?

Finally, good preparation sets the example for those who report to you. When your followers see how much you value your superior's time, they will begin to value your time as well. You can't create a culture of preparedness if you don't demonstrate a culture of preparedness. Ruddy Giuliani states, "Creating reasons for those who work for you to establish their own culture of preparedness is part of being a good leader."[19] It works the same when you're the follower. Know what your leaders *want* to hear from you and know what your leaders *need* to hear from you. And then give it to them, efficiently.

Build Relationships

Building a relationship with your leaders is very important. You need to know what drives them. You

---

[19] Giuliani. 65.

need to understand what keeps them up at night. You need to be able to read their body language, earn their trust, and speak their language. This doesn't necessarily mean that you become 'best buds', but it does mean you get to know what's important to them and how they think.

Communication is key to any job role. Your ability to communicate effectively with your superiors is critical both to your success and theirs. As an example, there was a time when it was my responsibility to turn a small technology manufacturing company around. The business was in a slump and had only one customer with a decent contract for custom engineered solutions that was about to be completed. Once the contract was finished, the company would have no source of income.

I developed a turnaround plan that consisted of creating new opportunities with the existing customer, as well as developing a series of new product lines. The product development, product marketing, and brand building efforts were going extremely well. We were building strong brand recognition in the target market and had developed a series of new products that were being very well received by early adopters.

The efforts to create new opportunities with the existing customer were also going extremely well. We had identified multiple new projects that we could help the existing customer complete. These new projects, combined with the growth of the new products marketable to a larger base of customers, had provided positive sales growth and a tremendous pipeline of future potential sales that had never existed for this company before. The company was now in a position in which it was poised to turn from bleeding to thriving. Because of the implantation of the turnaround plan, the business remained profitable after the existing contract finished. In fact, profitability was on the rise because sales had increased, and new process controls had improved operational efficiency. At this point, there were also several customers instead of just a single customer. The single existing customer had awarded us multiple new contracts that more than replaced the expiring work.

Despite all this success in developing the business, it takes time for that development to mature into a positive impact on the bottom line. Much of the profitability gains were being reinvested in product development and operational process improvements, so the net profitability hadn't yet shown signs of growth. The Board of Directors was unhappy. They couldn't see the positive growth that was taking place and the improvements that were being implemented to better ensure the future health of the business. All they saw was the bottom line that wasn't improving. Why? Because I hadn't communicated effectively, and they didn't see the bounty that was coming.

I ended up leaving that company with several years' worth of sales backlog already booked. This backlog would yield significant growth to the bottom line over the next few years, even if nothing new was done during that period. I had invested all my energy into the business, without investing enough energy into building a relationship with my superiors, the Board of Directors, so that I could communicate effectively. That lesson was a powerful one for me to absorb.

Building a relationship with superiors shouldn't be about edging into the "insider's club" or learning how to manipulate your leaders. Mr. Useem states, "Nor is leading up a call for undermining authority or seizing power. It is about the effective exercise of power for the greater good."[20] Building a relationship with your superior is a tool for adding value to your superior, to the organization, and to the mission. As you increase your understanding of your superiors, you will recognize both their strengths and their weaknesses. This, along with a strong knowledge of your own strengths and weaknesses, will allow you to best support your superior and add value to their efforts.

So, what does a good relationship with your superior look like? It begins with trust. It is essential that you demonstrate to your leader that you are worthy of trust. You do this by delivering on promises, avoiding office politics, never participating in office gossip, demonstrating loyalty, keeping confidential information confidential, and never being afraid to tell the difficult truth.

Good relationships are also filled with respect. Of course, you want your superior to respect you, and this means that you must demonstrate respect for your superior. I already stated that you should never participate in the gossip that is ever-present in offices, and there are also times when you need to step in to put a stop to it. When you overhear someone complaining about something the leader did (or didn't do), you should speak up about the value of giving the leader the benefit of the doubt.

Sometimes, it may also be wise to talk to the leader about the concerns within the ranks and coach your leader on the value of talking through the action or decision that has created concern for people. In this way, you provide an opportunity for your leader to better communicate and build support for the direction. This adds value and will ultimately

---

[20] Useem. 2.

be appreciated if delivered in a positive and supportive tone.

A noted exception to this would be in cases where your leader is moving in unethical or illegal directions. Never follow in that direction, and never defend such actions to others. It doesn't do any good to participate in gossip, even if the gossip is true. If the offense is such that it needs to be reported to proper authorities, such as legal authorities or the next level up on the org chart, then do so swiftly and honestly. But do not participate in office gossip because that will only cause harm.

Loyalty to the Mission

Loyalty to the mission is critical. You know your superiors are rewarded based on performance towards the mission, so whatever you do to propel the team in that direction is going to be of benefit to them as well. Your loyalty to the mission will also be manifested as loyalty to the leader. The exception to this is the case in which your leader has no personal loyalty to the mission. In such cases, maintaining loyalty to the mission is still the best approach because it will be noticeable to other leaders. You may want to begin the process of looking for a new leader to report to before the leader with no vested interest takes you too far in the wrong direction.

No mission will succeed without the loyalty of strong leadership and strong implementers.

In general, your leader is going to be loyal to the mission of the organization and your loyalty to this same mission is going to be highly valued. "Without loyalty, soldiers would not survive combat or continue to give their all each and every day to ensure mission accomplishment," states a columnist in the *Recruiter Journal*. [21] First of all, please let me say "thank you" to the brave men and women serving the mission of liberty in the armed forces. For most of us in business, "surviving combat" is proverbial rather than literal because we will never face the life and death battles that those in our military may face on our behalf, to protect our Constitution and the liberty it guarantees. Yet, the need for loyalty to the mission is just as valid in any organization. No mission will succeed without the loyalty of strong leadership and strong implementers. You have the opportunity to be both a strong leader and a strong implementer as you demonstrate loyalty to the mission that adds value to your superiors.

Leading Customers

Serving our customers well should be one of our highest priorities. And, as I've already pointed out, great leadership is about serving those that you lead, as well as serving your mission. Your customers buy from you, not so much for what you are selling, but for who you are and the mission that you serve. Your mission is important to your customers, and when you serve that mission well, you are serving your customers well.

Ken Blanchard teaches, "In high performing organizations, everyone passionately holds and maintains the highest standards for quality and service from their customers' perspective."[22] The entire organization is built around the mission, and the customer is at the core of this mission.

Principles for Leading Customers:

Customer First

Customer Centric Mission

Customer Centric Operations

Customer Centric Organization

---

[21] Clemmons, Sgt. Maj. Willie. "Leadership and Army Values Are Inseparable." n.d. *The Recruiter Journal*. USAREC Command. Web. 1 April 2016.

[22] Blanchard, Ken, Jesse Stoner and Scott Blanchard. "Serving Customers at a Higher Level." In Blanchard, Ken. (2007). *Leading at a Higher Level*. (39-63). Upper Saddle River: Prentice Hall. 39.

Processes, procedures, accountability, and measured key performance metrics are focused on the customer. You never build out processes and procedures just for the sake of having a process and procedure. Instead, you carefully design and implement processes and procedures that will add value and efficiency and serve your customer.

A major part of serving your customer involves influencing your customer – the very definition of leadership. Your efforts to influence your customer must be focused on the mission in such a way as to benefit your customers and add value to them. You guide them to understanding their needs, and how you can offer them solutions. If, and when, you learn that those solutions don't meet their needs, you either change your solution, or you guide them to a solution provided by someone else that is a better fit.

There is a scene in the 1947 film, *Miracle on 34th Street*, in which Kris Kringle, playing the role of Santa Clause in Macy's, tells customers where to buy products that Macy's doesn't have. His supervisors are upset and fire him, but Mr. Macy is thrilled because the store has received hundreds of letters professing undying loyalty to the store willing to send shoppers to competitors to ensure that they have happy customers.[23] Mr. Kringle was soon back on the job!

We must cultivate a culture in which the customers' needs are more important than our own. We may lose a small sale here and there, but we'll gain passionately loyal customers that return to us time and again because they know that we serve them first. To lead your customers well you must serve them better than anyone else.

---

[23] *Miracle on 34th Street*. Dir. Georg Seaton. Perf. Edmund Gwenn. 1947. <https://www.youtube.com/watch?v=IKfBUUhFueI>.

Leading Yourself

You cannot effectively lead anyone else until you are able to lead yourself. Leading yourself is about consistency and character.

Be Prompt

For instance, I've worked with leaders that will call meetings and will routinely be late for the start of that meeting. This is a combination of poor time management and disrespect for the team. Bill Hybels said, "Promptness is about character, and leaders are not beyond the rules that govern things like courtesy and character."[24] Leaders with poor time management skills show that they aren't effectively utilizing their time (or that of their team members who are attending the meeting). Being late is also disrespectful. For it sends the message that the leader's time is more valuable than everyone else's. On the other hand, when a leader is consistently early for the start of a meeting, it provides an opportunity for brief "check-in" conversations. This shows team members that not only is their time valued, but also that they, too, are personally valued.

Principles for Leading Yourself

Be Prompt

Be Courteous & Respectful

Be Proactive & Take Action

Be Courteous & Respectful

Of course, no matter how much a leader values other people, there will be times when mistakes are made or when circumstances beyond the leader's control cause the leader to be late. When this happens, it is essential that the leader apologizes for being late. First thing! Note that I said apologize, rather than provide excuses. The reasons may be accurate and valid. But, it is significantly more important for the team to know and understand that you value them and their feelings, more than your

---

[24] Hybels. 200.

need to provide a reason for your tardiness. I previously mentioned how Bill Hybels links promptness with character, and how he provides instruction on how people with character should act when they cannot get to a meeting on time. He further comments on the subject: "Anyone can give a valid reason why they're running a bit behind. But it takes grace and relational intelligence to keep that reason at bay until you've first let the group members know that their feelings rank higher than your justification."[25] This turns your mistake into a show of respect.

You also need to respect your team and colleagues. This requires self-discipline and genuine care for others. Show your team that you respect them by checking in with them from time to time. I don't mean checking in on how they are doing at their jobs. I mean asking how their vacation went, knowing who their spouses are and asking about them, and knowing their children by name and asking how they are doing in school. Sending the family a note or a gift card when a team member is asked to work longer than usual hours is also courteous. I remember sending a team member on a trip to Africa when his wife was pregnant. I realized that she would be worried about his safety while he was on travel, so I let her know that I would be traveling with him and that we would have armed escorts, and travel insurance that would provide a private jet ride home in the case of a health emergency. When we returned, I sent her a handwritten note via mail (not delivered to my team member but addressed to his wife). The note expressed my gratitude for her sharing her husband with the business, and a gift card for a day at the spa.

---

[25] Hybels.

Do make sure the families of your team know how much you appreciate them. This means not only asking your team members about how their families are doing but also personally telling the families "thank you" every now and then. It also means celebrating and grieving with them. Celebrate births, weddings, birthdays, and anniversaries. Recognize graduations, recitals, championships, and any other noteworthy events in the lives of your teammates' families. You may attend some of these events, but the most important thing is to recognize them. To recognize them, you must know about them. To know about them, you must ask.

Equally as important, perhaps even more important than the celebrations, are the sad times. Make sure you attend funerals of immediate family members. Always send flowers, or other condolences when you don't attend. The *US Army Leader Transition Handbook* states that when taking on a new leadership role, the leader should "Quickly learn the names of your subordinates and their spouses. Be aware of weddings, births, graduations, etc. Always visit your Soldier's civilians or family members who are in the hospital. If they sense you have a genuine concern for their personal well-being, they are apt to be more open and loyal."[26] You might not think that military leadership would invest time and effort into such things, but they know how important courtesy and respect are for building loyalty and passion. This message can be easily translated into business relationships as well. When you genuinely show courtesy and respect for your team, they will be loyal and diligent. When the time

---

[26] Reider, Col. Bruce J., ed. *Army Leader Transitions Handbook.* Combined Arms Center - Center for Army Leadership, n.d. Web. 8 Apr 2016.

comes for you to ask more of them, they won't hesitate.

Doing all of this requires you to manage yourself, and your time, wisely. Find a process that works for you, so that you can keep up with the things that are important to your team members. Take notes on things going on in the lives of your team members and their families. Follow up with them on a regular basis. Your follow-ups can't be contrived or impersonal. They must be sincere and from the heart.

Be Proactive & Take Action

Self-leaders are also self-starters. They don't wait for someone to tell them what to do. They observe others' needs and then act upon when they find them. It has been said that "An organization filled with self-leaders is an organization with an empowered workforce."[27] This is because self-leaders are proactive. Great followers are trustworthy and dependable. When you give them an assignment, they will handle it effectively. But, a self-leader won't wait for you to give them an assignment. They know the mission and will seek out ways to participate in the accomplishment of that mission. Consider the following example of taking out the trash, as simple and mundane as it might seem. A dependable follower will take out the trash every time you ask. However, a self-leader will make sure you never have to ask. Be a proactive self-leader that acts before being asked.

> A dependable follower will take out the trash every time you ask. A self-leader will make sure you never have to ask.

---

[27] Fowler, Susan, Ken Blanchard and Laurence Hawkins. (2007). "Self- Leadership: The Power Behind Empowerment." In Blanchard, Ken. *Leading at a Higher Level*. (103-116). Upper Saddle River: Prentice Hall. 105.

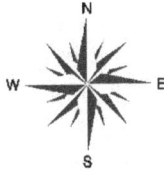

Leadership Process

Why do we desire to lead? Is it a thirst for power, a desire to help others, an interest in seeing things to completion, or a passion for a mission? Regardless of our reasons for wanting to lead, being a leader means being influential. In other words, a leader is capable of having an effect on people. That effect may be positive, or negative. I'm sure you can think of leaders that lifted people up to be more than they thought possible. You can probably think of leaders that took people on horrific paths of destruction.

For great leaders the effect that they have on people positively influences them to be more, to be better, to improve and grow and learn and contribute at a higher level. A leader effects the behavior of those they influence. A leader affects the development of those around them. A leader can even influence the character of others. A great leader drives behavior that improves relationships and results, intentionally develops people, and inspires a higher character ideal that people will strive to live up to.

What is the underlying mechanism that makes positive influence possible? How does a leader cultivate the level of performance that is desired? How does the leader effectively influence others? Throughout my years of providing leadership, I have developed a six-step process designed to teach leaders how to influence others, and act as a guide to continuously improve that influence. I didn't develop an understanding of this process overnight. There were many failures and lessons-learned along the way. It is an empirically derived process build on personal experience and the application of the concepts over years of leading teams. This process will show you how to go from being a good leader, to become a STAR Leader™. The process begins with defining your destination – your vision. This is what will inspire people to follow you.

Six-Step Process for Effective Leadership

Effective leadership requires six basic steps:

1. Create and cast a vision.

2. Build the proper team for realizing this vision.

3. Observe the state of the team.

4. Ask questions.

5. Adapt to the environment.

6. Influence those around you.

Step 1: Vision Casting

The first step in influencing others as a leader is to develop a vision. In my previous book, *Strategic Leadership*, I described the Vision Vector™ concept. When you strive to provide a positive influence, you must begin with an end in mind. That 'end' is your vision. The Vision Vector™ defines this vision in a manner that is easily talked about and understood by those you are endeavoring to influence or lead. The Vision Vector™ is simply a direction for your vision (the mission), and a magnitude defining accomplishment of the vision (the objectives). To lead effectively, you must begin with the end in mind, clearly communicating the mission to your team, and defining the objectives that will result in success.

Step 2: Team Building

The next step in the leadership process – the process of influencing others - is team building. This is where you ensure you have the right people on the team. You want people who are excited and passionate about the mission, and that either possess the skills or can develop the skills needed to accomplish the mission. You'll also want to clearly define the roles needed to accomplish the mission and make sure that the right people are in the right roles. Often, great people are mismatched and thus perform weakly. To lead effectively, you must know where you're headed, the kind of help you'll need to get there, and whom you can recruit to provide that help.

Step 3: Observation

The third step in the leadership process is observation. You're observing your team in action and looking for potential conflicts, relationship issues, personal challenges, learning styles, personalities, and development levels. These are the things that can impact team performance – positively or negatively. Strong leaders study, know what to look for, and then proactively observe.

Learn how to spot a brewing conflict before it boils over into problematic or destructive behaviors. Learn to identify someone's learning style and personality, so you can communicate with them more effectively. Be aware of everyone's skill level and lead accordingly. In the sections that follow, I'll address much of this in greater detail.

Step 4: Question

The fourth step in the leadership process is to question everything. Some might believe that steps 3 and 4 should be combined by noting that questioning is a method of observation. However, I have separated questioning from observation and have designated it as its own step. Why? Because our observations drive our questions, and those questions will either lead us to the next step or loop us back to do more observation. Questions also have application to more than just observations. A good line of questions can drive an audience in a particular direction or guide them on a path of self-discovery. You may, or may not gain new information, but your team will have made leaps that they may not have otherwise made.

In *Strategic Leadership*, I described the use of *Socratic Questioning* in coaching. This tool is extremely helpful in a variety of settings and is a vital tool for carrying out the "Question" step in the leadership process. Use questions to develop an understanding of your team, of the problems they face, and of the challenges of the mission. Coach your team to think through their challenges and consider alternative solutions.

Step 5: Adapt

The fifth step in the leadership process is adapting. This may mean changing your leadership approach. It may mean altering operational processes to improve efficiencies. Adaptation can also include changes to the team, such as training, mentoring, adding new people, re-organization of roles, and, at times, eliminating team members.

To adapt, you must understand yourself, each individual team member, the collective team, the mission and associated challenges. The sections in the remainder of this chapter describe the key elements of adaptation that a leader needs to have at their disposal. Study them closely and repeatedly. Proactively put them into action, practice them, and adapt how you implement them until you find what works best for you.

- Agile Tactical Adaptability™ describes a tool for identifying experience levels, priorities, and risk tolerances, and utilizing this information to adapt how you lead

- Learning and Communication Styles provides tools for identifying how to best communicate with your audience

- Asking Questions shares different types of questions that can be used

Step 6: Influence

Influence is achieved when you gain the confidence of an individual or a team to believe in the mission and strive for the objectives.

The process I've just described is not necessarily a 'stage-gate' process, in which each step is treated like an independent stage that must be completed prior to moving on to the next. Rather, the leadership process is more agile in nature in that implementation must be flexible and parallel. In other words, while it is helpful to think about the leadership process in terms of a linear series of steps, the truth is that these steps will typically be taking place simultaneously in any given leadership effort.

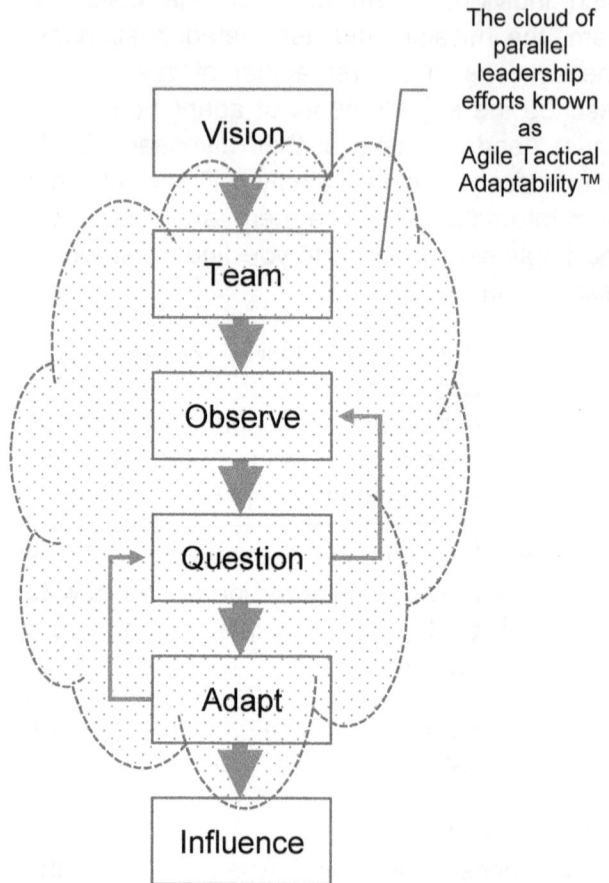

Figure 2. Leadership Process and the Cloud of Agile Tactical Adaptability™

You will be continually building and developing your team, observing, questioning, and adapting, to achieve positive influence that adds value by completing the mission. Creating a vision is an initial 'gate', and, once through this gate, your leadership process will more likely resemble a complex cloud of simultaneous activity. I call this cloud, the process of Agile

Tactical Adaptability™, as described in the following sections.

Agile Tactical Adaptability™

The only constant in life is the presence of change. Because situations, challenges, markets, environments, moods, communication styles, available information, attitudes, stresses, and other factors influencing organizational behaviors and performance are in a continual state of flux, great leadership requires a high level of agility and adaptability – it requires *agile tactical adaptability*.

Being agile is being nimble, rapid, and graceful in making necessary changes. It means you are decisive and able to think through situations quickly to draw conclusions. Tactical activity is action that is carefully planned and executed to achieve a very specific and clearly defined objective or situational advantage. Adaptability is the ability to adjust to changing situations or differing conditions.

Agile Tactical Adaptability™ is the ability to gracefully assess a situation, rapidly draw conclusions, and decisively adapt or change your tactics to suit the situation.

Agile Tactical Adaptability™ is, thus, the ability to gracefully assess a situation, rapidly draw conclusions, and decisively adapt or change your tactics to suit the situation.

Agile Tactical Adaptability™ means that a leader must read a situation, then apply the appropriate leadership style. The style of leadership is based on several factors, including urgency and importance of the mission, as well as the experience level of the one being led.

For example, more thorough leadership may be required when a team member lacks experience and needs greater direction and oversight. On the other hand, the more experienced team members are at performing a task, the less direction and oversight they will need. In fact, when those that follow you are experts in their fields, you may only need to accentuate the goal or objective. You will be amazed at the creative and innovative way they pursue the goal if you let them handle it on their own.

Years ago, I was managing a team of maintenance technicians. I knew what was needed to accomplish the mission, but they were the experts who would get it done. As their leader, I set goals for process improvements and reduced downtime, and then empowered them to come up with the plan to get there. The result was even better performance than the goals that I had set. They used their creative abilities to find innovative ways to ensure that the manufacturing processes ran at peak performance. We reduced downtime and increased production yield. Product was being produced at a faster rate, and with fewer defects. This meant we'd have few customer complaints, less scrap, more product to sell, and lower manufacturing costs.

Had I taken a more authoritative approach as a leader, the experts would have done exactly as I directed, and the innovative (and more effective) solutions they created would not have been realized.

This process of innovation wasn't perfect, however. Some of the ideas the experts envisioned didn't work. Together, we would discuss their ideas, talk through the risks of implementation, share those risks with the production team, and then decide on how to proceed. On a couple of occasions, we determined the risk was too high, and failure would result in longer than acceptable equipment downtime. These ideas were taken off the table, at least until we could come up with a way of mitigating the risk. Many times, the ideas were implemented, and failure resulted. Throughout the process, I would work with the team members, by observing and questioning, to help them learn from those mistakes. The results would often be a revision of the original idea or a different approach, which ultimately led us to the improvements that exceeded our expectations.

Leadership Styles

The most effective leadership style in any given circumstance will vary depending on the urgency and importance of the circumstance and on the maturity or experience level of the follower. The effectiveness of the application of any leadership style will also depend on the experience of the leaders themselves.

Urgency and importance are a critical component in determining the most effective style of leadership to handle a given situation. Often, when a task is extremely urgent and highly important, a strongly authoritative leadership style is the best choice. In life or death situations, taking the time to coach or mentor followers may simply be too costly.

For instance, consider a fireman entering a burning building where people are trapped inside. This fireman is not likely to take the time to evaluate if you have experience in such situations. He will simply take command and speak with authority to communicate what he needs you to do to maximize the likelihood of getting you safely out of the building.

Perhaps a better example might be a police SWAT team or a military special forces team. The team members know one another extremely well, and yet when they are in a potentially hostile situation, they have a predefined and highly authoritative hierarchy that must be followed, without exception. To break this hierarchy in heat of the battle puts lives in danger. However, during training exercises, when the risks of failure are less extreme, coaching will be a much more prevalent style of leadership.

Similarly, when importance is high, but urgency is low, the option to adopt more democratic leadership tactics is much more feasible because the cost of failure is more acceptable. In fact, it is during these situations that we develop leaders around us so that when the urgent situations do present themselves, we will have a pool of highly skilled leaders to rely upon when handling the emergencies.

Experience Levels

In *Strategic Leadership,* we reviewed the *work maturity (situational) model* of leadership. This model accounts for the variations in leadership style that are needed based on the maturity level of the follower. It identifies four leadership styles [delegating, supporting, coaching, and directing], and four levels of development [D1-D4].[28] For the concept of *agile tactical adaptability*™ (ATA™) in leadership style, I draw heavily upon the ideas presented in the situational theory, including the four styles in the toolbox, as well as varying levels of experience and capability (i.e. development). The details of each of the four leadership styles in ATA™ is adjusted slightly to include urgency and importance, as well as follower maturity in the task at hand.

A multi-level approach to defining levels of development is not new. Historically, the concept has been used for millennia in craft industries which designate levels, such as novice or beginner, apprentice, journeyman, master, and master trainer or grandmaster. In the popular *Star Wars* films, we see the levels of the Jedi order labeled as youngling, padawan, apprentice, knight, master, and grandmaster.[29] In karate, there are beginner kyu levels, advanced kyu levels, sempai dan levels, sensei dan levels, masters (Kyoshi), and a grand master (Hanshi). The Six Sigma quality philosophy borrows from the karate ranking using yellow belt, green belt, black belt, and master black belt graduations. Finally, in the Situational Leadership™ model, we see the enthusiastic beginner, disillusioned learner, capable but cautious performers, and self-reliant achievers.[30]

As an example, I am a student of Ueshiro Shorin-Ryu, which uses a three-level system of green belt, brown belt, and black belt, with

---

[28] Blanchard, Ken, et al. (2007). "Situational Leadership II: The Integrating Concept." In Blanchard, Ken. *Leading at a Higher Level*. (87-102). Upper Saddle River: Prentice Hall.
[29] "Jedi". Wookipedia. Web. 16 Sept 2016.
[30] "Situational Leadership II: The Integrating Concept."

graduated interim levels in between to label the experience levels of participants. A white belt is a novice – you're a white belt the moment you step foot into the dojo. The green belt is earned gradually – first with a single green tip on the white belt (known as ro-kyu), then with a second green tip (known as go-kyu), and finally a full conversion to a solid green belt (known as yon-kyu). Similarly, the green belt earns brown tips (known as san-kyu), then a solid brown belt (known as ni-kyu). Likewise, the brown belts will earn black tips (known as ik-kyu) before formally joining the ranks of black belts (known as sho-dan).[31] This progression is similar to the novice (white belt), apprentice (green belt), journeyman (brown belt), and master (black belt).

Once students reach the black belt rank, they become teachers in the general classes, and they also gain passage to a new "master's club", which are classes for black belts only. In this "master's club" of black belts, the learning scale starts over: The black belt is the novice instructor, the Sensei is the apprentice instructor, the Denshi is the journeyman instructor, and the Kyoshi are the master instructors – with a single grandmaster as Hanshi.

Now, to further explain the concept of ATA™, we will borrow from the karate ranking to differentiate experience levels. The White Belt is for a novice, the Green Belt is an apprentice, the Brown Belt indicates a journeyman, the Black Belt indicates a master, and Sensei for a grandmaster or teacher of teachers. All the while, please keep in mind that at any level there

---

[31] Scaglione, Robert and William Cummins. *Shorin-Ryu Okinawan Karate Question and Answer Book*. Person-to-Person, NY. 1984. 78-79.

is a spectrum of experience – just as the "tip color" shows the gradations which designate progress to the next level.

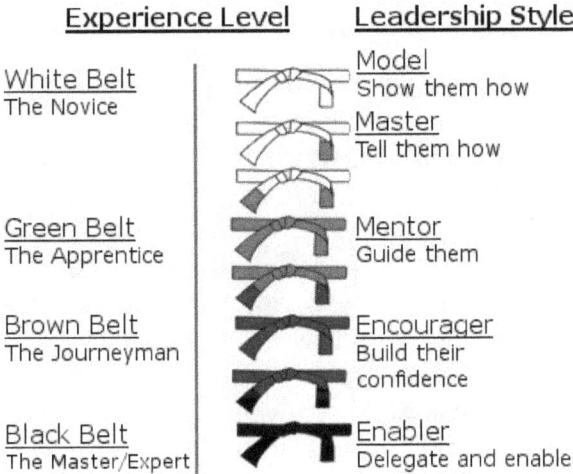

Figure 3. Experience Levels and Leadership Styles for
Agile Tactical Adaptability™

Using this system, for every task or specific responsibility, the experience level is different. In other words, individuals may be a "Black Belt" in one area while they are a "White Belt" in another. Today, in tech companies, it is very common for very talented and experienced engineers to be promoted to management roles. The problem with this practice is that the advancements are made with little or no leadership training; thus, the expertise that makes these engineers "Black Belt" product developers do not advance their skills in leadership, project management, or operations management.

Unfortunately, many organizations kill productivity because their Black Belt designers are no longer designing. Rather, they have shifted into leadership and management responsibilities with only a White Belt level of expertise. These engineers need a Black Belt in leadership and management to guide them as they transition into leadership and management roles. Then they will be better equipped to lead and develop new Black Belt engineers.

As this multi-level approach to leadership styles is implied in the craftsman and karate levels – and even in the fictional Jedi Order – it is also clearly defined in the Situational Leadership model.[32] A master craftsman will interact with an apprentice in a manner that is very different than the interaction with a journeyman, or fellow master. Just as a brown belt in karate teaches some concepts to the lower ranks while receiving detailed instructions on new materials being learned, and the finer points of things already learned, from the higher ranks.

While keeping in mind the belt ranks to signify experience levels in the ATA™ concept, we will use the nomenclature of Master, Mentor, Encourager, and Enabler to describe the discreet leadership styles available for use in this discussion. Keep in mind, that just like the experience levels, these styles have blended variability in between the discrete levels of the nomenclature. In other words, as experience allows, the leader can adjust to some level in between styles, such as using a bit of the Master style, while gradually moving towards the Mentor style at a pace suitable for a specific situation.

---

[32] "Situational Leadership II: The Integrating Concept."

The Model

When leaders act as models, they perform a task themselves while intentionally directing followers to observe and learn. However, this leadership style is one that you will want to use sparingly. It's like giving baby food to a child. You certainly don't want a teenager to not be able to eat solid food, so you must move past the little jars of mashed food as soon as possible.

There are, however, circumstances when leaders would find that specific modeling style to be effective. For example, when a follower is performing a complicated task for the first time, it may be best to see how it is done by observing someone with experience. Using a personal example: Not too long ago, the roof of our home took some damage from a hurricane. There was no structural damage; only about a ten-square-foot section of shingles were missing. I'm not a roofer, by any stretch of the imagination, but, thanks to the internet, it is relatively easy to find roof repair videos. In fact, some of these videos are made by excellent teachers that walk you through each step. Now, I was totally clueless about how to remove damaged shingles or lay the new shingles, so this kind of modeling was essential. I repaired the roof and it never leaked. However, without the modeling, I'm certain I would have had a leaky roof.

The Master

The Master leadership style is characterized by a highly autocratic and authoritative leadership methodology that provides very detailed directions on what to do and how to do it. A White Belt has little, if any, knowledge on how to properly complete the task or fulfill the responsibilities of the role, and, therefore, needs a Master to provide direction and detailed instruction. The Situational Leadership™ model calls this the "directing style" and notes that it is necessary when the development (experience) level is very low. I agree with this completely and would add that the Master leadership style may also be needed when a more experienced individual is faced with a catastrophic emergency.

A Master is a proven expert, one who directs and controls. The Master is in charge while the White Belt follows directions. Sometimes, however, this type of direction is considered as micromanagement. Mastering involves providing detailed instructions and monitoring the important details very carefully. I tend to think of micromanaging as excessively monitoring even the most unimportant details and refusing to let go and give the learner the opportunity to fail. White Belts can be offended by this level of oversight as well, and it can impede their own growth and development. Or, the wise beginner will embrace the oversight that maximizes their learning and potential for success. The White Belt who embraces the Mastering will quickly gain skill and transition to the Green Belt level and will no longer require Mastering, but, instead, Mentoring.

The karate dojo is an excellent example of this. The class is arranged with the students standing in order of rank. This isn't a means of building pride. It's a means of establishing examples. The highest-ranking students in the class will form the first line, with the next lower ranks in the line behind them, and so on until the beginners form the back line. This allows every member of the class to have an example directly in front of them that has more experience. The Sensei will stand at the front of the class or walk around and observe. This observing provides the Sensei the opportunity to offer "corrections" to the students. These "corrections" are simply coaching on how to improve. A White Belt will receive the most basic of corrections, such as "Place your feet here," "Step there," or "Imitate the row in front of you." This feedback will be "mastering" in nature. More experienced students will likely receive more detailed corrections on the precision of movements, breathing, stepping first, or rooting down into the stance. Some of it may be of a mastering nature, but much of it will be more mentor than master. The beginner will hear the more advanced students getting those corrections but won't know what they mean until they've been around the dojo for a while.

When a crisis or emergency occurs, it is generally best for leaders to transition from Master to Model, doing the tasks at hand themselves, while the White Belt observes. When failure is an acceptable learning experience, the leader should provide Mastering, but when that failure will be catastrophic to either the White Belt or the organization, the leader should stop mastering and start modeling.

Green Belt

The Mentor

While the Mastering style involves providing detailed instructions and oversight to followers, the Mentoring style consists of advising, counseling, supporting, and directing, when needed. While Mentors provide some direction, they tend to lean more towards support and counseling, rather than providing detailed direction and oversight. The Situational Leadership model refers to this style as the coaching style.[33] While I understand this choice of terminology, I do not prefer it because I believe that coaching is a much broader concept. There are times when coaches are highly directive, times when coaches must step back and simply mentor, and still other times when they delegate responsibility. I personally believe that everyone, at every level, needs a coach to help them maintain peak performance. For this reason, I avoid using the term "coaching style" and prefer to use the term Mentoring.

As we discussed earlier, the Green Belt is an apprentice who looks to the Mentor for more advanced development. In the karate dojo, the green belt is referred to as the *backbone of the dojo*.[34] Green Belts are experienced enough to assist with teaching, responsible enough to help with maintaining the dojo, eager enough to desire more training, but can sometimes become disillusioned by the increasing difficulty of the skills they are learning.

The same is true in any organizational role. Green Belts begin to become efficient in their roles but haven't mastered them yet. They will take on more responsibility and may even be helpful in showing the ropes to the White Belts. But, at times, the Green Belt will be overcome by the increasing complexity of tasks and responsibility, and thus the Mentor will need to

---

[33] "Situational Leadership II: The Integrating Concept."
[34] Scaglione, Robert and William Cummins. *Shorin-Ryu: Okinawan Karate Question and Answer Book*. Person-to-Person Publishing, 1984. 78.

step in and provide some counsel, a little direction, and a lot of encouragement.

If a crisis emerges, leaders should revert to the Master style. The Green Belt is experienced enough that the leader should not have to step in and take over completely. However, when failure is not an option, leaders must provide more direction and closer oversight than would usually be given to someone with Green Belt-level experience. Clear communication is essential during such times. It is important to let the Green Belt know that your increased level of direction and oversight is not a reflection of a lack of trust. Instead, the severity and criticality of the situation calls for any caring leader to provide more than the usual amount of direction and oversight to maximize the Green Belt's potential for success.

Remember that in a karate dojo the student will line up by rank so that the more experienced students provide an example for the new students to follow. In a traditional dojo, there is even more to it than this. In ancient times, dojo existed to secretly train everyday citizens to be warriors when needed. This practice dates all the way back to the Shaolin monasteries where the martial art originated. These monasteries were well run, self-sufficient islands of agricultural efficiency. As a result, bandits and war-lords would often invade the monasteries to steal the food that the monks had prepared.

The monks trained in the martial arts every day, simply as a means of survival and defending their homes and their livelihood. They had a similar method of lining up by rank when practicing their martial arts, and the highest ranks would always be closest to the doorway.

This was so those with the most experience would be closest to the fight if invaders attacked during the training. If attacked, these more experienced martial artists would instantly drop mentoring and mastering, and become the model by being the first to the fight. They didn't want to risk failure by letting the inexperienced warriors be first to the fight.

Green Belts must choose for themselves how to react to this oversight. If they view it with resentment, they can hinder their growth. If they view it with enthusiasm, it becomes an opportunity to see how the leader handles such difficult and urgent challenges. This type of leadership is a spectacular learning experience for Green Belts, providing them with the potential to teach lessons and develop growth.

Brown Belt

The Brown Belt is an experienced journeyman that has demonstrated skills and the ability to handle many challenges with very little oversight. Leadership will often lean on the Brown Belt to help with Mentoring and Mastering. The Sensei may lead the Brown Belt with the Encouraging style in most situations but may act as more of a Mentor, occasionally even Master, to the Brown Belts role as Master or Mentor to less experienced team members. This is how you develop leaders around you. Delegate leadership and lead the leader in a manner that is fitting for them. They may have a great deal of experience in their official role, but very little experience training others to fill that role.

The Encourager

Brown Belts generally do not require detailed instructions (Mastering) and will not need formal Mentoring. Instead, Brown Belts require an Encourager that intentionally reminds them that they have the skills necessary to get the job done on their own. Leaders should lightly delegate to Brown Belts, entrusting them to get the task done, while still verifying that it has been properly executed. This idea has been around for as long as there have been leaders. In fact, it is codified in the axiom "Trust but Verify", which had been made famous by President Ronald Reagan when he was negotiating with the Soviet Union.[35]

In emergency situations, the leader of a Brown Belt will revert from Encourager to Mentor, increasing the level of direction to maximize the potential for a successful outcome. As always, the Brown Belt has the choice to react positively or negatively to the increased level of mentorship and direction. A negative reaction will result in resentment and cause the leader to lose respect for the Brown Belt's experience. This can become a roadblock to further personal growth and development.

On the other hand, positive reactions demonstrate the Brown Belts' humility and devotion and will increase a leader's respect for, and trust in, them. Brown Belts grow and develop through experiences such as these, adding "black tips" to their experience level, and moving them closer to mastering their roles.

Black Belt

Black Belts are masters. They do not generally need Mastering, Mentoring, or Encouraging. However, they will require

---

[35] As an example, see this press release conducted by Ronald Reagan and Mikhail Gorbachev. Web. 6 Apr 2016. <https://www.youtube.com/watch?v=As6y5eI01XE>

Enabling. When leaders are Enabling a Black Belt, they are delegating tasks and responsibilities entirely to the Black Belt. They are also working behind the scenes to ensure that the Black Belt has all the resources needed to succeed. They know that once a task is delegated, the Black Belt will get it done. Leaders don't need to verify the results, partially because they have full faith in the Black Belt's capability. They also know that the Black Belt is experienced enough to follow up with their leaders by providing status updates to keep them informed on progress.

The Black Belt will also typically be given new roles, often with increased leadership and management responsibilities. In these new roles, the Black Belt may be a White Belt. This means that while the leader can delegate some tasks to this Black Belt, other tasks will require more direction and oversight. Usually, Black Belts can also be White Belts, Green Belts, and Brown Belts in a variety of other roles and responsibilities.

ATA™ model can be summarized using the experience levels, priorities and behavior styles as follows:

The STAR Leader™ is highly skilled at recognizing these variable experience levels in the individuals that they lead, and in adapting their leadership styles as Master, Mentor, Encourager, and Enabler. In fact, the leader will be a Black Belt in certain areas and White, Green, or Brown Belt in other areas.

When leading Black Belts during an emergency, it is best to revert to an Encouraging style. This provides them with more support and serves as a reminder that they can handle the crisis. Often, we fail unnecessarily because leadership doesn't provide the encouragement that drives passion. Even the most experienced masters in their fields are flawed humans that will experience self-doubt. A great leader recognizes this and provides encouragement when needed. Brown Belts need steady encouragement on a continual basis, and Black Belts will need encouragement when faced with a crisis. When a leader provides the encouragement needed during high-intensity situations, Black Belts are energized and motivated to live up to their leader's assessment of their capability. It's unlikely that they will let you down.

Table 1. Leadership Behavior Styles

Model	Do the task yourself while followers watch and learn.
Master	Provide detailed instructions and close supervision.
Mentor	Provide some direction while giving preference to support, counsel, and advising.
Encourage	Provide little, if any direction. Focus efforts on a more supportive role that encourages followers to trust their own abilities.
Enable	Delegate tasks completely to followers, and work behind the scenes to ensure that they have the resources needed to enable success.

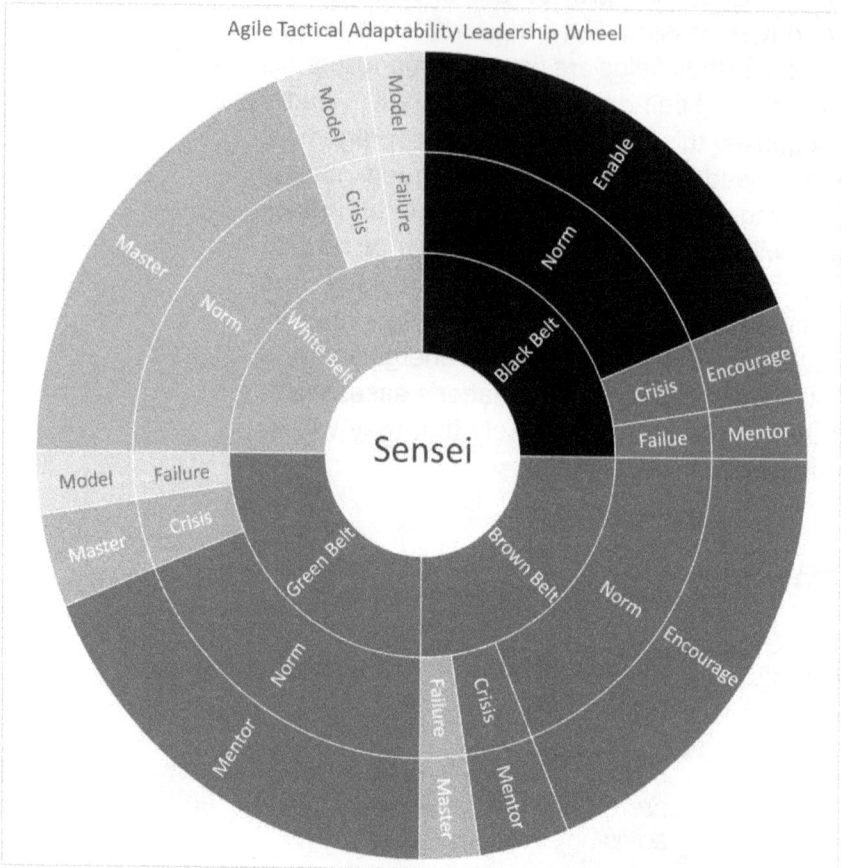

Figure 4. Agile Tactical Adaptability Leadership Wheel™:
Experience Levels, Urgency, and Leadership Styles

The ATA Leadership Wheel™ depicts leadership styles applicable to each experience level, including times of crisis or significant failure. Located in the center is the leader or Sensei. The innermost ring is the experience level ring for each of the Sensei's team members; however, it is important to note that everyone on the team, at every belt level, can, and must, be a leader. The second, or middle, ring is the urgency level. It is assumed that every situation represented has a high importance (anything not important shouldn't be on your radar anyway). Regardless of the importance, the urgency may vary. At each development level, the main urgency level is "normal" with two other urgency levels possible – crisis, and failure.

We've already mentioned how crisis situations likely warrant a step back in leadership style. However, this may not always be the case. As you step back, you may quickly learn that your team members have things under control. If not, remain on the lower rung of the leadership style ladder.

Failures along the way are to be expected. Failure is a part of the learning process. Nobody is perfect, and if there was a perfect somebody, you would be reporting to them rather than the other way around. However, some failures are costly for the organization and/or bad for your followers' morale. To help them recover quickly, you will need to revert a notch or two on leadership styles.

When leading a Brown Belt at journeyman-level that experiences a significant failure, for example, you will need to step in with Mentoring. As you do so, evaluate the situation and discern quickly if you need to act as a Master for a brief time as the failure recovery is taking place.

For example, remember the example I provided from my own career in which I defended and engineer that had made a mistake that set the project back. This engineer was a Brown Belt on the team. He didn't need a lot of hand-holding, but after this failure, he did need more mentoring than usual. I mentored him specifically on how to solve the problem and communicate that solution effectively to reduce the likelihood of a recurrence. He didn't need a

Master to give him a detailed to-do list, just a Mentor to provide a rough sense of direction and coach him through the process. It didn't take long to get this failure behind us, and as soon as it was appropriate to do so I reduced the Mentoring that I was providing and moved more into Encouraging.

Take great care of the individuals you are leading during this process. Jumping in with Mastering without providing the Encouragement of a strong explanation of your intent to help them recover and learn from their mistakes may cause an even greater morale problem. This would result in a leadership failure stacked upon an operational failure. While you may recover the operations, you may lose a valuable team member (or at least lose a lot of potential for growth in that team member).

Use every failure as an opportunity to teach and to learn. Let the team member know that you are stepping in to help and that you will take the blame for their failure. After all, part of the root cause may very well be that you didn't supply the resources needed or the encouragement needed for them to perform well. Don't misunderstand me on this. I'm not recommending that you don't hold the person accountable. What I am recommending is that you save the accountability for after the recovery. In other words, recover from the failure in both the operational setting and in the individual morale of your team members. Then, once the recovery has been made or is well underway, hold them accountable in an appropriate manner. Make sure they understand that you support them, even as you hold them accountable for the failure.

Learning & Communication Styles

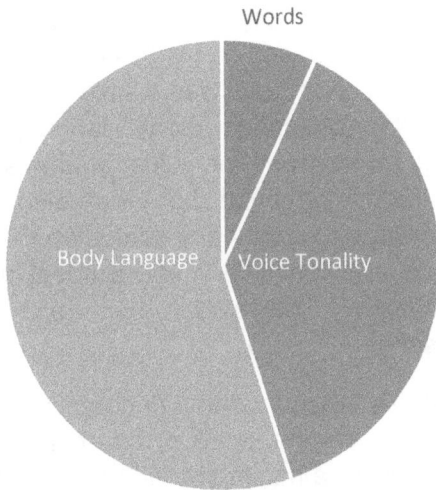

Good communication is essential to leadership. You must be able to communicate vision, you must be able to communicate important information and details, and you must be able to communicate through the often-ambiguous social interrelations within a team. Everyone communicates in different ways. Knowing and understanding this can help you to be a better communicator and, thus, a better leader.

Communication

Words

Body Language

Voice Tonality

Figure 5. Relative Significant of Types of Communication

In any communication, the actual words make up a small fraction of the meaning conveyed or perceived. In fact, words account for only seven percent of the meaning, while voice tonality drives 38 percent of the meaning, and body language a whopping 55 percent. The words are the content, and the tones and body

71

movements determine how the content is received. They can clarify or mislead.[36] This is why face-to-face communication is so much more effective than email or text messaging, and why using your senses, not just your words, to communicate effectively enhances your ability to get your point across.

As an example, I remember receiving an email about some interpersonal conflicts that I needed to address. The email contained wording that gave me a rather negative perception of how things had been handled thus far, which left me feeling uneasy and disturbed, to say the least.

After meeting with the person that sent the email and discussing the email face-to-face, I realized that a significant portion of my perception was based on my misinterpretation of the wording. Not only was I able to reap the benefits of observing body language and listening to the tone of voice of the speaker during the conversation, but I was also able to ask questions to clarify any confusion that I had regarding the conflict. My perception was tremendously adjusted by a simple conversation.

For this reason, when I'm coaching leaders on effective communication, I remind them to keep emails to a minimum and use face-to-face communication as much as possible. This reduces the risk of them being misunderstood, and it also increases their ability to gain knowledge and insights that they would not get otherwise.

---

[36] O'Connor, Joseph and John Seymour. (2001). *Introducing NLP: Psychological Skills for Understanding and Influencing People*. San Francisco: Conari Press. 16-17.

A process known as neuro-linguistic programming (NLP) provides you with a set of tools to communicate better by building strong rapport with your audience, developing improved sensory awareness, establishing an "outcome thinking" mindset, and enhancing your behavioral flexibility. In fact, these four elements (rapport, sensory awareness, outcome thinking, and behavioral flexibility) are considered the "pillars of NLP."[37]

Rapport is simply a relationship in which the parties involved understand one another and communicate well. Specifically, we're looking for the development and application of "approaches for building rapport and influencing others."[38] *Behavioral flexibility* refers to the adoption of "techniques for developing personal flexibility and awareness of others."[39] *Outcome thinking* is simply the development of "strategies and approaches for self-motivation and the motivation of others."[40]

The *sensory awareness* portion of the NLP concept provides for the idea of sensory or learning modes as a component of learning styles. "These *modal preferences for learning* are only a small part of what most theorists would include in a complete package deserving

---

[37] Ready, Romilla and Kate Burton. (2010). *Neuro-Linguistic Programming for Dummies*. Chichester: Wiley. 13.

[38] Carey, John, Richard Churches, Geraldine Hutchinson, Jeff Jones and Paul Tosey. (2010). "Neuro-Linguistic Programming and Learning: Teacher Case Studies on the Impact of NLP in Education." CfBT Education Trust. 11 Web. 19 Sept 2016.

[39] Carey, et al.

[40] Carey, et al.

to be called a *learning style*."[41] The learning modes include the acronym VARK:

- Visual

- Aural (Auditory)

- Read/Write

- Kinesthetic

Care must be taken not to put too much emphasis on the learning modes. One's preferred mode is simply an indicator of how one most prefers to learn. It does not convey anything about how effectively one learns or the quality of one's learning or communicating. "VARK tells you about how you like to communicate. It tells you nothing about the quality of that communication."[42]

In surveys of first-year medical students, it was found that most students preferred material taught in multiple learning modes. In fact, 63.8 percent of those surveyed preferred multi-modal teaching, over any single mode of teaching, to optimize their retention of the material.[43] Of those preferring multi-modal teaching, 43.4 percent prefer all four of the VARK learning modes to be used in presentations.[44]

---

[41] Fleming, Neil and David Baume. (2006). "Learning Styles Again: VARKing up the Right Tree!" *Educational Developments 7.4*, 4-7. Web. 4 Apr 2016.

[42] Fleming and Baume.

[43] Lujan, Heidi L. and Stephen E. DiCarlo. (2006). "First-Year Medical Students Prefer Multiple Learning Styles." *Advances in Physiology Education 30.1*, 13-16. Web. 4 Apr 2016.

[44] Lujan et al.

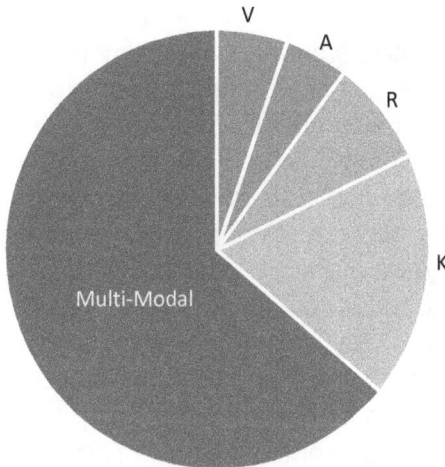

Figure 6. Preferred Teaching/Learning Modes

As portrayed in the pie chart, those claiming a preference for a single mode were most likely to choose kinesthetic (just over 18% of the total population), followed by reading/writing (7.8%), visual (5.4%), and auditory (4.8%).[45] This is critical to know and understand because most of us naturally use just one or two of the learning modes as we communicate. Think about what this data suggests about that. If you are communicating in just one mode, you are communicating inefficiently (and maybe ineffectively) somewhere between 82 and 95 percent of the time. If we proactively learn how to communicate in those modes that don't

---

[45] Lujan et al. It is important to note that this data is based on student's' responses to questions on a survey. This means the data is subjective, rather than objective. It is based on student opinion and perception, not on statistically validated actual results. I would think that validated results would most likely indicate a much higher percentage of multi-modal learners; perhaps, even 100 percent (this statement is also opinion; a perception that has not been validated).

necessarily come naturally to us, and intentionally apply all the learning modes as we communicate, we will become significantly better communicators.

It is also a premise of NLP methodology that there are techniques known as "mapping" that enable one to identify the preferred learning or communication style of the person being addressed. If true, this is a powerful skill to develop because it will not only empower you to identify the preferred modality of your audience but also help you adapt to it as you communicate with them. Be careful, and don't forget that most people prefer multi-modal communication as the best means of helping them grasp the material you wish to communicate. This means you should be intentionally using all the modes. Still, for many individuals, one mode will stand out as the strongest, or dominant mode. Having the ability to identify this during a conversation, and adapt to it, will enhance your ability to communicate.

There are several types of "mapping" that we can use to help us identify the dominant mode of our conversation partner. The validity of these mode-mapping models is not statistically verified, yet still may be of practical help. It is left to the reader to put these mapping models into practice and make a personal determination as to the effectiveness and helpfulness in everyday communication.

The first mode mapping model is language mapping. Its premise is that the language that one uses to communicate provides a clue into the dominant mode of learning for that individual. For instance, one who is dominant in the visual mode may prefer visualizing what is taking place, 'taking a peek at information,' 'sizing up a problem', or saying, 'I just can't see it'. One who is dominant in the auditory mode may use language like 'it sounds like this is taking place,' or 'this is what I'm hearing from you,' or 'it's just falling on deaf ears.' A kinesthetic dominant person may use language like 'I'm starting to get a handle on it,' or 'I can't quite put my finger on the problem,' or 'I need to touch the issue to better understand it.'[46]

Another mode mapping model is eye mapping. This model suggests that you can infer a person's dominant learning mode by observing the movements of their eyes during conversation. Research studying individual eye movements during cognitive tasks has indicated that "people tended to look in the opposite direction of the part of the brain they were using to complete a cognitive task."[47] The eye-mapping model suggests that those who are dominantly visual learners will move their eyes up and towards the right, or up and towards the left when they are thinking [right and left are from their perspective, not yours]. Someone who keeps their eyes level while moving to the right or left, or those who move their eyes down and to the left, are likely dominant in the auditory mode. And those who move their eyes down and to the right, when thinking, are generally dominant in the kinesthetic mode.[48,49,50]

---

[46] Shipper, Stephanie. (1995). Building the Field of Dreams... Building Relationships that Enhance Peak Performance/Productivity (presentation note handouts). Durham: Expert Outcomes.

[47] Dilts, Robert. (1998) "Eye Movements and NLP." *NLP University*. NLPU.com. Web. 19 Sept 2016.

[48] Dilts.

[49] Fowler, Barry. (2015). *FSB Business Coach Training Manual*. Section 3.09. Fowler School of Business.

[50] Shipper.

As a personal example, I've noticed that I usually look down and to the right when I'm thinking, but will, on occasion, look up and to the right instead. According to the eye mapping model, this suggests that I'm dominantly a kinesthetic learning, with some strong visual learning tendencies as well. I would tend to agree strongly with this assessment of how I like to learn. Once, early in my career, I was doing a presentation when an executive in the company asked a question that required me to carefully think through my response. I paused for a few seconds and glanced down and to the right while thinking. This executive declared to the room that my pause indicated that I didn't know what I was doing. I was totally embarrassed, which I think was his intent, but managed to bounce back by explaining that my response to his question needed to be carefully worded because the complexity of the situation made misunderstanding easy and I wanted my response to clearly articulate what he was looking for without any ambiguity. That opened the door for me to draw him a picture – literally, on the whiteboard. Thankfully, he was a visual learner and my picture helped him understand. If I had known about NLP then, I could have been more intentional about explaining in multiple learning styles from the beginning.

Breathing and speech patterns are also a mapping model for learning modes. Those who are dominant in the visual mode tend to breathe from the high chest with shallow, quick breaths, and they speak quickly (just like the executive in my example above). Auditory dominant learners tend to breathe from the mid-chest and speak rhythmically. Kinesthetic learners tend to breathe deeply from the diaphragm, with slow, methodical breaths with pauses in the timing and will speak in a similar pattern of slow, thoughtful words with pauses for reflection as they talk (this is my natural way of communicating).[51]

The mode mapping techniques are wonderful tools to keep in your toolbox, however, I must admit that I have used them with mixed results. There have been times when utilizing these techniques have helped me adjust my method of delivery or presentation when I was struggling to get my point across. After making adjustments, the person with whom I was speaking often started to understand what I was trying to communicate. In other instances, I've either not been able to map someone's dominant mode, or my attempts to adjust to the perceived dominant mode failed to improve my ability to get through.

This personal observation seems to align well with critical research. One author states that "NLP offers a highly pragmatic and accessible approach to communication and people development that can help with a wide variety of needs for effective performance, change, and learning."[52] A few sentences later, that same author states, "Contrary to what many NLP practitioners espouse, NLP is based on theory, but that theory is poorly articulated.... The field lacks a thorough evidence base."[53] With this in mind, note that NLP can be a powerful tool for improving your ability to communicate and influence (e.g. to lead), yet it should not be

---

[51] Fowler, Barry. 3.10.
[52] Tosey, Paul and Jane Mathison. (2009). "Chapter 1: Introduction." In *Neuro-Linguistic Programming: A Critical Appreciation for Managers and Developers*. NY: Palgrave Macmillan.
[53] Tosey and Mathison.

approached as the perfect tool that will solve all of your communication problems.

The mode that works best for any given individual may also vary. My son, for example, tends to be a kinesthetic learner, whereas my daughter is a visual learner. However, there are times when the hands-on approach just doesn't work with my son and providing him with a picture or a written description is more helpful. Likewise, there are times when pictures don't work with my daughter but using something she can touch, and feel will better get a point across to her.

For instance, drawing pictures to illustrate math is often a good way for me to help my daughter understand her homework. Recently, I did this while trying to explain the concept of fractions. It wasn't working, so I went and got an apple. After cutting the apple in quarters, I handed her a piece. As she held the piece of apple I explained to her that she was holding ¼ of an apple, and asked her how many quarter-apples did she need in order to have one whole apple. As she picked up the pieces, I could see the illumination on her face. Handling the apple helped her to understand the concept of fractions. Even though she is quite dominantly a visual learner, in that moment she needed to touch and feel the problem in order to understand it.

In general, I've found the best results while intentionally using multiple modes of communication and utilizing the mapping techniques when difficulty arises in getting my point across. Sometimes it helps; sometimes it doesn't; having the tool available to try will at least give you a place to start and provide valuable flexibility that will benefit your communication.

ILS Communication Tool

Another way of looking at learning styles is by categorizing learners on a continuum scale: Active versus reflective, sensing versus intuitive, visual versus verbal, and sequential versus global.[54] This scale is known as the Felder-Silverman scale, named for the researcher who first proposed it, Richard Felder and Linda Silverman.[55] It is assessed using the Index of Learning Styles (ILS) developed by the authors.[56] It is said that individual preferences will rest somewhere on a scale between each extreme, and that "Your preference for one category or the other may be strong, moderate, or mild. A balance of the two is desired."[57]

Active learners tend to learn by activity, such as discussion, application, or explaining concepts to others, while reflective learners prefer to think over the new concepts quietly to process and absorb them.[58]

Table 2. ILS Learning Style Dimensions[59]

Dimension	Style Continuum
Perception	Sensory – Intuitive
Processing	Active – Reflective
Input	Visual – Verbal
Understanding	Sequential – Global

---

[54] Felder, Richard M. and Barbara A. Solomon. "Learning Styles and Strategies." n.d. NCSU. Web. 4 Apr 2016.
[55] Felder, Richard M. and Linda K. Silverman. "Learning and Teaching Styles in Engineering Education." (1988). *Engr. Education, 78(7)*, 674-681. With author's preface (2002). Web. 19 Sept 2016.
[56] Felder, Richard M. and Barbara A. Soloman. *Index of Learning Styles*. NCSU. Web. 19 Sept 2016.
[57] "Learning Styles and Strategies."
[58] "Learning Styles and Strategies."
[59] Felder and Silverman.

Sensing learners prefer to learn via well-established methods. They dislike surprises or complication and tend to be very patient with the details. Intuitive learners, on the other hand, tend to like discovering all the possibilities. They won't like repetition, and they will be better at quickly grasping new concepts. The sensing learner is very process-oriented, while the intuitive learner is more innovative yet may not focus enough on processes that provide efficiency.[60]

Visual learners prefer pictures, diagrams, flowcharts, and timelines, while verbal learners prefer written or spoken explanations.[61]

Sequential learners tend to gain understanding in linear steps that are arranged in logical order, while global learners tend to learn in chunks – a bit here, a bit there, and then, seemingly all of a sudden, the connections between the chunks take shape and they start to "get it."[62]

Use of this tool can be as simple as maintaining an understanding of the various learning style dimensions and developing an awareness of the preferred styles with those whom you are communicating. Through practice, you will develop skill at adjusting your communicating methodology to mirror the preferred learning style of your audience.

In other words, be observant to how people perceive information, how they prefer the input of new information to be formulated, how they

---

[60] "Learning Styles and Strategies."
[61] "Learning Styles and Strategies."
[62] "Learning Styles and Strategies."

process information, and how they develop an understanding of situations. By making these observations, you empower yourself to adjust your communication methodology to improve the effectiveness of your communication with any individual.

Just as with the VARK model, this model simply recognizes differences in how people absorb information and attempts to describe these differences in terms that are quantifiable, descriptive, and helpful. Recognizing that people learn in different ways and need a variety of ways for information to be communicated, is an essential step in transforming from good leader to STAR Leader™.

Questioning Everything

Asking questions is one of the steps in the leadership process that takes place after the initial vision and before the resulting influence. Knowing how to ask the right questions is also a handy tool that leaders can use to successfully guide, develop, and influence. In fact, you'll use this tool during every step in the leadership process.

Questions are a powerful tool for exploration, for focused probing, for changing minds, and for guided discovery. Previously, I referred to the use of Socratic questioning as a method of discovery. In *Strategic Leadership*, I described the six basic types of questions used in Socratic questioning: clarifying questions, probing assumptions, probing reasons and evidence, questioning viewpoints and perspectives, probing implications and consequences, and asking questions about the question.[63]

This description of the types of questions involved is helpful, yet it provides very little insight into how to apply these questions in productive practice. Here, I would like to address a conceptual approach to application. It is not my intent to provide you with a list of questions. Instead, I want to provide an explanation for the reasons behind the questions, so that you will develop a fundamental understanding of the process, rather than simply memorizing a list of questions that you may not properly understand how to apply.

In application, Socratic questioning is a systematic approach using questions to reach some end: exploration, focused probing, changing someone's mind, or guiding someone's discovering of a solution. This "systematic questioning involves the use of a graded series of questions designed to facilitate independent thinking."[64]

Questions as a tool for Exploration

Questions can be used to explore general information about an individual, a concept, or a situation. Such exploratory questions are used to develop a better understanding of the situation, to illuminate an individual's values, to identify where clarity exist or where it lacks, "or to uncover problematic areas or potential

---

[63] Thompson, Justin. (2016). *Strategic Leadership*. Viera, FL: 2Xalt Press. 95-97.

[64] Overholser, James C. (1993, Spring). "Elements of the Socratic Method: 1. Systematic Questioning." (67-74). *Psychotherapy*. American Psychological Association. 30(1). 67.

biases."[65]   Any of the six types of Socratic questions may be used for exploring.

Exploratory questioning may be useful during conflict resolution.   Whenever a team exists, conflict is inevitable. We tend to think of conflict as inherently bad, however, the truth is that some level of conflict can be beneficial. If no one ever disagrees, there is no debate or discussion about which is the best path to take to move forward.   Yet, individuals come with biases, preconceived notions, and assumptions that will impact the conflict. Using questions to reveal these biases and assumptions can help manage the conflict and guide the discussions to a fruitful and beneficial outcome.

Exploratory questioning may also be useful when building your team.   This includes team member selection, task assignments, and creating development plans for team members.

Consider the situation in which your team has been assigned a new project. You will need to determine the level of knowledge and understanding among team members, as well as assess everyone on the team. How much does the team know about the project? Do they have the technical details necessary to successfully complete the project? Use exploratory questioning to determine if your team can handle the project, if additional training is necessary to enable your team to succeed, and who should take the lead.

Sometimes you'll already know the answers to these questions. Yet, I've found that it is often

---

[65]   Paul, Richard and Linda Elder. "Critical Thinking: The Art of Socratic Questioning, Part III." *J. of Developmental Education.* 31(3). 34-35.

helpful to ask questions for which we think we know the answers anyway. By asking questions, we get people thinking about the answers. We may also find those answers to be different than what we initially believed. In this sense, the Socratic questioning methodology becomes a means of discovering our own biases and assumptions, as well as the team's.

Questions as a tool for Focused Probing

Focused probing, like exploratory questioning, helps you explore the unknowns among your team. Exploratory questions look to expose issues or biases. Focused probing drills into the issues or biases to find a solution to the issue or a way around the biases.

Perhaps there is a lack of trust or a misunderstanding between two members of the team. Once this is discovered, focused probing can be used to dig deeper into the issue and begin the process of resolution and reconciliation. If you don't take the exploratory step first, you may not understand why the conflict exists in the first place. This may cause you, in turn, to make improper assumptions about the conflict, and thus make improper decisions about how to handle it.

Furthermore, using exploratory questions to identify an issue allows you to target the root cause, rather than just the symptoms. A more focused probing of the root-cause can guide the team members to see other perspectives, alternative solutions, express their own assumptions, and consider the implications and consequences of their stance on the issue.

Questions as a tool for Changing Minds

Questioning may also be used to guide an individual, or a team, to see things from your perspective. This is a powerful leadership tool for guiding a team, or individuals, to adopt your vision as their own. When you are trying to convey a vision to others, you can take the autocratic approach by stating the vision and demanding that the team get on board because that's their job. Or, you can share your vision with the team using the question and discussion approach, where you ask questions that guide the team to understand the reasons for your passion about the vision.

The autocratic approach may work in some situations; however, with the question and discussion approach, you will yield more passion for the vision and greater loyalty to the cause. Because without passion and loyalty it will be much more difficult to succeed (especially in the long term)! The fact is, most people want to be passionate about what they are doing. When this passion is missing, they will lack internal motivation. As you may well already know, motivating with a big stick is never the best solution. When people see your passion and adopt the cause and vision as their own, you won't need to motivate them. They will have an internal passion that does all the motivating you need.

Care, however, must be taken with this approach. When you are striving to change someone's mind, to lead them to adopt your vision and perspective as their own, make sure you've considered the alternatives and are certain that your vision is the best vision to have. Use this approach to inspire passion in the vision but be careful when implementing the details of progress towards that vision. In other words, use this "mind-changing" approach to guide your team to see the value of the vision, but then allow them to determine how to make that vision a reality.

Any of the six types of Socratic questions can be used to influence the perspectives of individuals or teams. The key point is that you, as the leader, have an endpoint in mind for the discussion. The questions are merely tools for guiding that discussion in the direction you want.

Questions as a tool for Guiding Discovery

Guiding discovery is a process that leads others to discover something about themselves or an issue at hand. When you want to guide discovery, you do not have an endpoint for the discussion in mind. Instead, you guide the individual or team on a path to discovery. As you travel along together, what you find may be something you didn't even know yourself.

This process is used to guide others so that they can create a vision for themselves. Exploratory questions are used to uncover needs, desire, and interests. Focused questions are then used to guide others to create that vision and a plan for bringing that vision to fruition. Dr. Christine Padesky, a cognitive therapist, states, "In this more empirical process of (1) gathering data, (2) looking at this data in different ways with the client, and (3) inviting the client to devise his own plans for what to do with the information examined, there is discovery going on."[66] While Dr. Padesky's commentary

---

[66] Padesky, C.A. (1993, September). *Socratic questioning: Changing minds or guiding discovery?* Keynote, 1993 European Congress of Behaviour and Cognitive Therapies,

88

relates to therapists who provide cognitive therapy, her statement is also applicable to leadership coaching. I'm not suggesting that leaders or coaches are therapists in any way. Therapists treat psychological problems. If one of your team members suffers from such a problem (depression, anger management, etc.), do not – under any circumstances – attempt to be their therapist. Unless you are a trained and licensed therapist, you could inadvertently make matters worse.

However, every leader is part coach, and being a coach means that you must guide your team members to discover solutions for themselves. Dr. Padesky continues: "We are not simply fixing problems but also teaching ways of finding solutions."[67] Further, she defines Socratic questions, within the context of guiding discovery, as:[68]

A. Asking questions that the individual (or team) has the knowledge to answer

B. Drawing the individual's (or team's) attention to information which is relevant to the issue being discussed but which may be outside of the individual's current focus

C. Moving, generally, from the concrete to the more abstract so that...

D. The individual (or team) can, in the end, apply the new information to either

London.   p.   3.   Web.   19   Sept   2016.
<http:www.padesky.com/clincalcorner/>
[67] Padesky. 4.
[68] Padesky. 4. Reworded slightly, to change the frame of reference from that of a therapist/client discussion, to that between a leader (as coach) and the individual (or team) being led.

reevaluate a previous conclusion or construct a new idea.

The first part (A) of this definition asserts that coaching is not about pinning anyone to the wall. Asking questions that people can't answer is never helpful. Relevancy (B) defines the need to keep the discussion focused on what is important while guiding the team to see other perspectives or points that may have relevance, even if they haven't been considered up to this point. It isn't that you have an end in mind, but that you want to keep the discussion on point while broadening perspectives to include new ideas. Beginning your questioning with the 'concrete' (C) helps clearly define the issue or topic of discussion. As the conversation progresses, moving to more abstract questioning helps guide others to discover details on their own, and thus apply them independently (D).

The end goal is not to engage in problem-solving for your team, but rather to employ a systematic questioning approach to help them discover the solution on their own. You will not only end up with better solutions but also with a more confident team with developed problem-solving skills.

At this point, you may ask if there is anything more we, as leaders, can do to further develop our questioning methods. Perhaps these methods are new to you, or you wish to improve upon your own system of questioning. If so, consider Dr. Padesky's four-stage process of guided discovery:[69]

---

[69] Padesky. 5-6. I have listed Dr. Padesky's four stage process with my own comments to clarify its application to leadership.

A. Asking informational questions

Create a concrete definition of the issue to be addressed that is shared by everyone involved.

B. Listening

Listening may be the most important part of the discovery process, and, perhaps, the most difficult. "Listening is the second half of questioning. If you are not truly curious to know the answer, don't ask the question."[70] When you do not listen, you drive the process with your own biases and assumptions. To avoid this, listen carefully to the answers received. Listen also to the tone of voice, word choices, body language, emotions, and metaphors. Each of these will provide information in addition to the specific details of the answer provided. Is the speaker using positive language or negative?

C. Summarizing

Every so often in the discussion, time should be taken to summarize what has been covered. When you summarize the conversation, you insert a natural pause that provides time for ideas to settle. Pausing allows for a moment of reflection so that you can visualize the big picture and see how the content of the discussion fits into it. It's like stepping back from a puzzle while still holding several pieces in your hand. It's easier to see where these pieces belong when you can see the entire picture

---

[70]   Padesky. 6.

Pausing also helps you and your audience maintain the same level of understanding. When you summarize, it allows the individual or team to respond with an affirmation, a clarification, or a disagreement with that summary. You may have perceived a portion of the conversation differently than others. Thus, the summary allows time to correct that perception, if necessary. In this manner, pausing helps to avoid miscommunications and misunderstandings.

D. Synthesizing or analytical questioning

During a discussion, you may go through multiple rounds of questioning, listening, and summarizing. But, you'll also want to ask questions that guide the individual or team to make connections between the initial topic of discussion and the series of questions and summaries. Do the results or conclusions of your conversation affirm, or stand in opposition to original assumption or hypothesis regarding the issue? Be careful not to provide the connection yourself. Instead, ask the necessary questions to guide the team to discover the connections on their own.

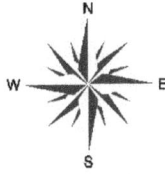

Leadership Practices

There are seven key leadership practices that every great leader must be intentional about applying every day. Each of these are "high level" practices that can be implemented in a myriad of ways. Being intentional and proactive about implementing these practices is essential for the STAR Leader™. These critical leadership practices are:

1. Champion the Foundation

2. Cultivate the Vision Vector™

3. Model the Mojo

4. Coach Performance

5. Build Unity, not Uniformity

6. Enable and Empower

7. Focus the Operation

In the following sections, we'll discuss each of these leadership practices along with some ideas on how to apply them.

Champion the Foundation

The foundation of a healthy organization rests on a strong purpose and solid principles. Championing this foundation means driving the purpose and principles deep into the culture of

STAR Leadership Practices

Champion Purpose & Principles

Cultivate the Vision Vector™

Model the Mojo

Coach Performance

Build Unity, not Uniformity

Enable & Empower

Focus the Operation

the organization. Just writing down a purpose statement and a list of values doesn't do anything for you. Of course, you must write them down, and you must passionately live them out and put them into practice.

Championing the foundation means driving the purpose and principles deep into the culture of the organization through clarification, communication, and instruction.

What is your purpose? Why does your team or organization exist? Does your team know this purpose? More importantly, does your team *own* this purpose? Writing down your purpose doesn't magically bring it to life. Your purpose must be thoroughly and incessantly communicated. Doing this will give your team a strong head knowledge about the purpose, but this still isn't sufficient. You've got to drive this purpose into their hearts by way of their heads. The head is the seat of understanding, and the heart is the seat of passion. It's this passion that will bring the purpose to life in your organization. Without it, you've just got a team of laborers. But with the kind of passion that comes from true believers in the purpose, you will have an unstoppable force.

Similarly, defining principles – though an essential first step – will do nothing to drive these values into the organizational culture. Once the principles, or values, are defined, they must be communicated. This communication does not take place during an annual meeting or discussion, it must be continually reinforced and incorporated into processes, procedures, and daily communication. To make this happen you must model your purpose, and intentionally drive it with proactive effort. The U.S. Army recognizes this drive for purpose: "You are the role model for the ethical and moral climate of the unit," its Leader Transition Handbook states. "Your example speaks for what is acceptable and what is not. Empower your Soldiers [your team] to do what's right both legally and morally."[71]

Still, you know as well as I that it's not enough to simply model the principles. You must preach them, enforce them, and reward those that live by them. Bill Hybels said, "Leaders must figure out what values they believe should be manifested in their organizations. And then put them over the flame of a Bunsen burner by teaching on those values, underscoring them... enforcing them, and making heroes out of the people who are living them out."[72]

This is how you champion your purpose and your principles. First, you define them, then you model them. You consistently communicate them and teach them. You underscore the foundation and reasoning behind them. You enforce them with consistent and fair accountability. And, perhaps, most importantly, you make heroes out of those who *own* them and passionately live by them.

---

[71] Reider, Col. Bruce J., ed. *Army Leader Transitions Handbook*. Combined Arms Center - Center for Army Leadership, n.d. Web. 8 Apr 2016.
[72] Hybels, Bill. (2008). *Leadership Axioms*. Grand Rapids: Zondervan. 55.

Cultivate the Vision Vector™

Vision Vector™

The Front Page:
Colorful imagery and strong communication

The Direction:
An inspiring mission

The Magnitude:
Well defined objectives

After pounding purpose and principles into the culture, the single most important leadership practice is creating and inflaming the Vision Vector™. Vision is your strategic intent. It is also seeing what others cannot. "It is a dream that has been fashioned and molded into an image that can be communicated to others."[73] A successful vision will inspire passion for the cause and a deep-rooted desire to see the vision come to life. "If you're working on something exciting that you really care about, you don't have to be pushed. The vision pulls you," says Steve Jobs!"[74]

Consider, for a moment, that your vision is like a newspaper. There is a "front page" containing attention-grabbing headlines and imagery, then there are sections of the paper that contain the real content. The "front page" of the vision is the verbiage that conveys the message of vision to an audience in colorful imagery. It grabs their attention and compels them to look deeper and learn more about this story.

The content of your vision is composed of two sections that are both summarized on the 'front page' and detailed in a strong mission and a series of objectives. We need a mission that unifies and inspires us while defining *what*. "A mission is a strategic assignment delegated to, and accepted by, an individual or team."[75] A strategic assignment provides direction, always

---

[73] Thompson, Justin. (2015). *STAR Performance*. Nashville: Westbow. 16.
[74] Jobs, Steve. *Foundation for A Better Life*. Values.com, 9 Apr 2014. Web.
[75] STAR Performance. 19.

answering the question of what we should be doing. In this way, mission is the directional component of vision.

Objectives provide us with something to aim for. They are the key desired outcomes of our efforts. They are where we desire to end up, or what we intend to accomplish, as we work on our mission. Objectives are then measurable and definable strategic targets. You cannot fully define a vision without providing objectives that define when the vision has been achieved. In this way, objectives define a magnitude for the vision.

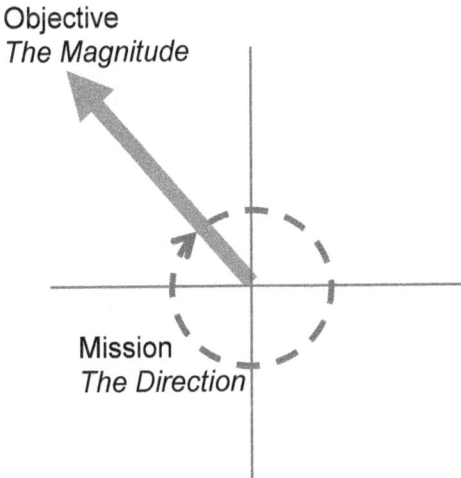

Figure 7 The Vision Vector™

A vector is a quantity used in math and physics to describe something with both magnitude and direction. For instance, speed is a scalar quantity because it only tells you a magnitude, how fast you are going, but velocity is a vector because it tells you how fast you are moving in a particular direction. Your Vision Vector™ give you a magnitude – a measurable outcome – and a direction – where you are headed. The objectives provide the magnitude that defines when the mission has been accomplished, and the mission gives the direction that tells you what you are working towards. This vision, along with its purpose and principles, must be driven into the organization. It must be incorporated into how you talk about the organization. It can't only be brought up in sales pitches, corporate briefings, and strategic planning sessions. You must model it as part of your everyday culture. When the team sees that you live and breathe the Vision Vector™, then they will live and breathe it as well. If they don't see this in you, you can't expect them to live it either.

Model the Mojo

This leadership practice is just about being in the game. Your *mojo* is your ability to be effective, to be successful, to stay positive, and to get things done in the face of challenges. To have a team with mojo, you've got to be a leader with mojo. You simply must model the behavior that you want to see from those on your team.

When change is needed – be that change. Eventually, your team will catch on, but it's only going to happen AFTER you model the behavior first. When challenges arise, be the first to step in and help so that you model a sense of urgency, strong teamwork, and support.

If you want your team to be passionate about the purpose and vision, then you must demonstrate passion and excitement for the purpose and vision. If you want a team that is steadfastly adherent to the principles of the organization, then you must model steadfast adherence to the principles. If you want a team that proactively solves problems, then you must model proactive problem solving yourself.

In general, your team will rise to the level of performance that you model. When you find individuals on your team that don't rise to this level, then you need to find out why or replace them. Just don't expect your team to perform at a level higher than you are willing to demonstrate yourself.

To gain the respect of their teams, it is important for leaders to build credibility. The best way to do this is to demonstrate competence. This requires taking action, setting the example, and getting things done. "Subordinates will respect a leader who is technically and tactically competent, willing to listen to their ideas and who leads from the front."[76] The following four keys help leaders to earn respect:

1. Technical competence,

2. Tactical competence,

3. A willingness to listen, and

4. Leading from the front, or consistently setting the example.

Technical competence is the demonstration of the fundamental knowledge and experience necessary to handle the responsibilities of the role you fill. If you lead an engineering team, you need to know a little about engineering, project management, systems integration, etc. If you lead a tax accounting practice, you probably need to be able to demonstrate competence in accounting and tax law. If you lead a company, you need to know a bit about what it takes to run a successful business.

---

[76] Reider. 19.

**Four Keys to
Gaining Respect**

Technical
Competence

Tactical
Competence

Willingness to Listen

Consistently setting
the example

Tactical competence is a working knowledge of how to get things done. It's the ability to put plans into action, understand people, align the organization, delegate appropriately, define and plan projects, and the like. Your team needs you to demonstrate an ability to accomplish things. Start with something small that will create a short-term win that is important to the mission and will be recognized as such. This will help you gain credibility with your team, and it will also boost morale. If your team sees a technically competent person that just can't get things done, you won't have their respect. As an example, consider your list of projects to do at home. How many half-done projects do you have around the house? Get 'em done! Be the model for seeing things through when you start them. Set the example that everyone on your team strives to live up to, in both your personal and professional life.

Another important part of modeling your mojo is time management. Punctuality tells people you value them and their time. As previously stated, being late for meetings sends a signal of disrespect and devaluation. "Time management is critical to your success and builds credibility with your subordinates. Prioritize, delegate and don't let crisis management monopolize your time. Providing subordinates with predictability builds credibility and trust."[77]

---

[77] Reider. 20.

Coach Performance

A STAR Leader™ must be more than a boss or a manager. A STAR Leader™ must also be a coach. To understand what being a coach means, think about the people that coach professional sports teams. In fact, most sports teams have multiple coaches. The head coach is responsible for leading the development of logistics planning and coordinating its successful execution during a game.

The head coach is also responsible for selecting the team members, and then guiding them to perform at their very best when it matters most. A coach, whether the head-coach or an assistant coach, provides encouragement when players are feeling discouraged, provides an "atta-boy for a job well done and calls people out when they don't give the team their very best. The coach helps every performer identify areas for improvement, set goals for performance, practice off the field, and perform on the field. The coach is part boss, part cheerleader, part vision caster, part manager, and all leader.

A coach is part boss, part cheerleader, part vision caster, part manager, and all leader.

These characteristics of a coach apply not only in sports but also to your leadership role within your organization. When you coach people, you are helping them excel. "Coaching educates team members and makes them capable of performing autonomously, thereby raising their efficacy."[78] You help your people identify areas for improvement, develop plans to get better, and set goals with tangible metrics that you then monitor. You encourage your team members when they are down, help them learn from their mistakes, cheer their successes, cast a vision that excites them, manage the logistics of team performance, resolve conflicts between team members, and organize the placement of people in specific roles and responsibilities.

Build Unity Without Uniformity

The idea of "unity without uniformity" is that of a team filled with diverse people who are all focused on the same mission and objectives. Uniformity is homogenous. A uniform organization, where 'everyone is the same,' is boring and useless. Just as useless as a football team that fields eleven quarterbacks and no running back, offensive linemen, receivers, tight ends, or other positions. They are going to get crushed.

The Apostle Paul paints a remarkable picture of unity without uniformity in reference to the Christian Church. He compares the Church to a human body, stating, "For the body does not consist of one member but of many" (1 Cor. 12:14)[79]. He carries this discussion to almost comical degrees, making the point that the body is not at all uniform in nature, yet the body acts

---

[78] Srivastava, Abhishek, Kathryn M. Bartol, and Edwin A. Locke. (2006). "Empowering Leadership in Management Teams: Effects on Knowledge Sharing, Efficacy, and Performance." (1239-1251). *Academy of Management Journal* 49.6. 1242.
[79] *The Bible.* The English Standard Version. Crossway. 2001.

in perfect unity. He states, "If the whole body were an eye, where would be the sense of hearing? If the whole body were an ear, where would be the sense of smell? But as it is, God arranged the members in the body, each one of them, as he chose. If all were a single member, where would the body be? **As it is, there are many parts, yet one body"** (1 Cor. 12:17-20, emphasis mine)[80].

Imagine your team as a body, just as Paul described the Church. You will have a variety of talents, skills, personalities, experience levels, and capabilities – *many parts*. Never let any member of the team treat another member as though they are unimportant, or unnecessary. Every member on your team is important, and every member can and must contribute to the overall success of the organization. Every member of the team, no matter how inconspicuous they may seem, has a very important role to play. These roles are the *many parts* of the body (team), and when they all work together in unison towards the same goals and objectives, you have unity.

When an engineer believes the salesperson is irrelevant, that same engineer will soon be out of a job due to lack of revenue. If the salesperson thinks the production associate is not important, the salesperson will soon have a lot of unsatisfied customers because the orders will be left unfulfilled. Production associates that look down upon the receptionist will soon find themselves unable to produce because they spend all their time answering the phones.

---

[80] *The Bible.* The English Standard Version. Crossway. 2001.

Celebrate and encourage diversity on your team. Rejoice in the variations of personalities that make team meetings so "sticky" because without these differences everyone would think the same; innovation would come to a standstill and conflict would escalate exponentially.

When a team is diverse, there will be a variety of ideas. When a team is in unity, those ideas will be sharply focused on what is important. The Apostle Paul's reference to the Church, which has unity without uniformity, continues, "If one member suffers, all suffer together; if one member is honored, all rejoice together" (1 Cor. 12:26)[81].

"If one member suffers, all suffer together; if one member is honored, all rejoice together" (1 Cor. 12:26)

This should be your team motto! When everyone is truly working in unity, they suffer together, but they also rejoice together. No one is seeking gain at the expense of another.

The key to unity is a clearly defined and articulated vision. Everyone on the team needs to know exactly what the mission is, and how they are to contribute to achieving that mission. When this is clear to everyone, everyone will be in unity.

---

[81] *The Bible*. The English Standard Version. Crossway. 2001.

Enable and Empower

Enabling and empowering is all about providing resources and opportunity. These words are very similar in meaning yet have some subtle differences that can be important. At the risk of stating the obvious, to enable someone is to make them able to perform some task. It means to provide the permission, the resources and the means to get something done. This word tends to focus on the provision of competence or ability, equipping and making ready for action. In order to enable someone to do something, we provide them with the resources, the means, and the permission to succeed.

Enabling focuses on providing the means

Empowering focuses on providing the power and authorization.

To enable someone is to provide the permission, the resources, and the means to get something done.

To empower someone is to give them the authority to do something. This authority is more about the transference of power and authority than about the provision of direction and resources. It suggests that the authorized are more powerful, stronger, and more confident than they were prior to the empowerment. When we empower someone to do something, we are, in effect, delegating power or authority over that task to them.

We are also giving them the power of learning by experience. Others have defined empowerment, in the context of leadership, "as behaviors whereby power is shared with subordinates and that raise their level of intrinsic motivation."[82] When we delegate power and

---

[82] Srivastava, et al. 1240.

authority to an "A player" on our team, the "A player" responds with increased motivation and excitement. "Empowering leadership is positively related to both knowledge sharing and team efficacy, which, in turn, are both positively related to team performance."[83]

The words "enable" and "empower" can be considered as synonyms; however, "enable" focuses more on providing the means, while "empower" focuses on providing the power and authorization.

Why is empowerment important? Over the years, research has shown "that the practice of empowering subordinates is a principal component of managerial and organizational effectiveness."[84] In fact, the efficient leadership of highly effective teams demands empowering the team to make decisions for themselves. This results in a team of leaders – a 'force multiplier' that expands the influence of leadership. The power and effectiveness of any organization are enhanced when power and control are shared throughout the organization.[85] This doesn't mean that the responsible leader abdicates responsibility or is overrun by committee. It means the leader takes responsibility by sharing the load and empowering team members to make decisions and execute them effectively.

[83] Srivastava, et al. 1243.
[84] Conger, Jay A. and Rabindra N. Kanungo. (1988). 'The empowerment process: Integrating theory and practice." (471-482). *Academy of Management Review*. 13(3). 471.
[85] Conger and Kanungo. 471.

Empower your team by transferring power
and authority to make decisions and drive
activities

Empowering your team – giving them the power and authority to make decisions and drive activities – is just the start. You must also enable them to execute on this empowerment. This includes providing both means and opportunity, and it also means adjusting the systems, processes, and procedures to back up the power you've provided. If the organization's systems, processes, and procedures don't back up the empowerment, then you haven't really empowered anyone to do anything. How do you do this? You design your organization and operation such that "company policies and cultures emphasize self-determination, collaboration over conflict/competition, high-performance standards, nondiscrimination, and meritocracy."[86]

You must give your team both corporate and individual opportunities to stretch their skills and abilities by trying new things. Enabling them in this way means that you give them the freedom to fail. Every failure is an opportunity to learn. If you want your team to learn, develop, and improve, you must allow them to fail. You want to provide the means to succeed, yet you must allow them the freedom to fail if they are to ultimately succeed.

You can't empower your children to ride a bicycle without enabling them to fall off. As a parent, you first hold the bike so that they will not

---

[86] Conger and Kanungo. 478.

fall. When the child gains confidence and learns to balance, you let go. You run beside them for a moment so that they do it themselves before realizing you're no longer holding them up. They'll panic and crash into the grass, then you'll quickly make sure that they are OK, and put them right back on the bicycle again. Every parent does this, and I did the same with both of my kids. I let them fail repeatedly – only stepping in to protect them if they were going to run into something that would cause more than a skinned knee.

If you want your team to learn, develop and improve, you must allow them to fail.

After a few crashes, followed by me forcing them to get right back on the bicycle, they started getting the hang of it. It didn't take long before they were cruising the neighborhood without any need for me to participate in the processes of their bike ride at all. To be honest, that feeling of exhilaration I experienced when I saw the look on my kids' faces as they rode by themselves for that first time is what excites me about leadership. That is exactly what "real world" leadership is all about. You must enable your team to succeed, which means you give them the freedom to fail AND you encourage them to try again when failure strikes. You may see frustration, and heartache, and even a bit of disillusionment at times. But, ultimately, you'll see people succeed and be filled with pride and excitement knowing that they did it themselves. Before you know it, they'll be teaching the task to the new guy or gal.

This is the push-pull nature of leadership. I mentioned earlier in this book that leaders must be out front, leading the charge. This is very true, and those who are too lazy or too afraid to be on the front lines will never be effective leaders. However, be careful not to use this as a reason to always do everything yourself. While much of leadership is about going first and pulling others along with you, there are times when great leadership requires that we push those we are responsible for. We push them to do more than they thought possible. We encourage them when failure strikes and push them to try again.

When my kids crashed their bikes, I encouraged them by checking their wounds and reminding them that, although learning to ride is difficult, it isn't impossible. More than once I literally had to pick them up and forcibly sit them back on the bike. I recall doing this once while my child was screaming and sobbing uncontrollably. They weren't hurt but were letting fear and panic control them. I thought to myself, "My neighbors are going to think I'm torturing this kid." While my child may have viewed it as torture for a moment, it wasn't long before they were yelling, "Look at me, Daddy! I'm doing it!" That's the *push* that every leader needs to be able to provide.

There are times, however, when the cost of failure can be too high. As I ran beside my kids before they had the confidence to ride alone, I would often let them fail, but occasionally the cost of failure was too high for me not to intervene. If a car backed out of a driveway in front of them, or if they began to veer off course towards a tree, I would step in and catch them or correct their motion. I'd let them crash onto the grass, or into the bushes, but I was not going to stand idly by and watch them run into a tree or get hit by a car. Instead, I used these times as "teaching moments" to help them understand why controlling their direction and using the brakes are important.

Likewise, when leading teams in such circumstances where failure is too costly to allow, it is important to involve the team to devise ways to achieve without failure. A higher degree of leadership oversight may be required to help the team (or individual) get through the challenge and learn in the process. In general, providing direction and then allowing the freedom for creativity and ingenuity in the execution of activities will result in greater gains in the long run. You will, almost certainly, experience losses due to failure in the short-term, and long-term success is rarely if ever, achieved without some short-term sacrifices.

Focus the Operation

Finally, a leader must take an intentional and proactive role in focusing the operation. All too often leaders define a purpose, clear principles, and both mission and objectives, yet they make no efforts to ensure that the operations of the business are aligned with and precisely focus on, these foundational elements.

For instance, are the compensations plans for the sales team aligned with principles set forth for the organization? If a fundamental principle of the organization is honesty, then the sales compensation plan better not be set up to implicitly encourage dishonest sales practices.

Whether implicit or explicit, your mission is going to involve satisfying your customers. Are your internal business processes aligned with your customers' needs? Do you have burdensome legal constraints, such as approving an NDA (non-disclosure agreement) with a prospect requires a month of review, thus hindering your sales team's ability to communicate with the prospect? Are your cost estimating and pricing processes efficient enough to allow your customers to receive timely quotes, or do you force them to wait longer than your competitors to complete a quote or estimate? When customers send products in for repair, do your procedures aid or inhibit communication with the customer?

The leader's responsibility is to focus all business operations (systems, processes, and procedures) on the mission. You want to do more than satisfy your customers; you want to turn them into *ecstatic* customers. Leadership expert Ken Blanchard says, "In high performing organizations, everyone passionately holds and maintains the highest standards for quality and service **from their customers' perspective.**"[87] It is the leaders' responsibility to set the example and keep the entire organization focused on this goal. Everyone in the organization must also work to create such a relationship with customers so that they will simply love doing business with you. This is true whether you are a B2B (business-to-business) supplier, a consumer products retailer, a nonprofit organization, a school, or any other type of organization. You must first determine your mission, which will define the kinds of customers you will serve. Then you must determine the expectations of those customers. And finally,

---

[87] Blanchard, Ken, Jesse Stoner, and Scott Blanchard. (2007). "Serving Customers at a Higher Level." In Blanchard, Ken. (39-63). *Leading at a Higher Level.* Upper Saddle River: Prentice Hall. (Emphasis mine.)

you must lead your organization to center every single process and procedure around exceeding your target customers' expectations. Any process that hinders the ability to exceed customer expectations should be refined to remove this hindrance, or it should be abandoned.

Bonus: Develop The Leader
Universal Lifelong Learning

Leadership development through a passionate commitment to lifelong learning is a bonus practice that creates long-term gains and continuous improvement. It is essential because the world around us in a constant state of change. The rate of change is faster today than it ever has been throughout history, and it will continue to increase in the future.

As an example, consider the technology we use to rapidly exchange information. Once upon a time, everything written was chiseled on stone tablets. The use of scrolls and forms of paper introduced a form of communication that was much easier to transport. Later, there was the Pony Express, then the railroad. Then along came a quantum technology leap: the telegram, followed by the fax machine, email, text messaging, and social media. Today, there may be times when it is still appropriate to use older technology to communicate. But, if you haven't learned how to use the newer technologies, you are missing out on modern-day modes of communication.

To keep up, leaders must be intentionally focused on continuously learning and promoting the development of those that they lead. Lifelong learning applies on both the individual and organizational levels. Individuals and organizations must both be learning new things as well as new ways of doing old things. Individuals accomplish this through study and practice, and organizations accomplish this with data analysis, communication, team building, and systems designed to promote learning and continuous improvement.

Organizations must have systems in place that record lessons learned so that mistakes are not repeated, and efficiency is improved over time. The top leadership experts of our day agree that lifelong learning and improvement, for both the individual and the organization, are essential. John Kotter said, "As the rate of change increases, the willingness and ability to keep developing become central to career success for individuals and to economic success for organizations."[88] His findings suggest that individuals that intentionally develop and learn over time will have more fruitful and rewarding careers. Likewise, organizations that are intentionally designed for continuous improvement will reap the rewards of greater economic success. Similarly, the first chapter of, "Leading at a Higher Level," addresses the topic of organizational performance. The authors state, "High performing organizations constantly focus on improving their capabilities through learning systems, building knowledge capital, and transferring learning throughout the organization."[89]

---

[88] Kotter, John P. (2012). *Leading Change*. Boston: HBR Press. 186.
[89] Carew, Don and Fay Kandarian and Eunice Parisi-Carew and Jesse Stoner and Ken Blanchard. (2007). "Is Your Organization High Performing?" In Blanchard, Ken. (3-19). *Leading at a Higher Level*. Upper Saddle River: Prentice Hall. 11.

It is important to note that developing leaders requires the commitment of both the individuals and the organization. To remain successful, organizations will need to become a place where leaders are continually developed, and organizational processes are strongly focused on the purpose, principles and passion inspiring vision. These organizational processes must be continually monitored and improved, and the leaders of the organization must be intentionally developed. Organizations that want to capture long-term success will absolutely need to be intentional about developing and incubating leadership at all levels of the organization.[90]

Three Types of Behaviors

Our behaviors are fueled by skills and capabilities and can be categorized as intrinsic, instinctive, or intentional.

Intrinsic Behavior

The word *intrinsic* refers to something that is part of the essential nature of something. When a characteristic is intrinsic, it exists as a natural part of that to which it refers. An intrinsic behavior is, thus, based on inherited skills and traits, and is a completely natural part of the individual.

Some things will just come naturally to you. With little or no effort, you can perform at a high level. No one will develop an expertise without substantial practice, yet expertise is much easier to develop for those areas that are intrinsic.

Malcolm Gladwell describes the process of developing these intrinsic behaviors as

---

[90] Leading Change. 174.

'capitalization learning,' or the process of getting better at something by building on our natural strengths.[91]   This is simply capitalizing on intrinsic behaviors – developing and improving skills that come naturally. You have a natural ability, and you practice it because improving in this area is much easier than improving in other areas.

Instinctive Behavior

An instinctive behavior is one that spins into action without any forethought.   This behavior drives action almost on autopilot. We don't even have to think about it; we just do it. These are the areas in which we have developed keen expertise.

Sometimes intrinsic behaviors become instinctive. This is generally because we tend to practice those things that come naturally to us, and this practice cultivates instinct. However, I must admit, there seem to be times when certain behaviors, skills, or capabilities come so natural to some people that these skills become instinctive with almost no effort. This isn't to say that such instinct will demonstrate an expertise. Yet, some people are so gifted in an area that they can perform better than most without even trying.

A behavior becomes truly instinctive when it is built on a great deal of practice. When we repeat a task many, many times, it will eventually become instinctive. This isn't necessarily due to intrinsic, or natural, ability.   It is simply memorized and forced into our subconscious through repetition.

---

[91]   Gladwell, Malcolm. (2013). David and Goliath: Underdogs, Misfits, and the Art of Battling Giants. NYC: Little Brown. 112.

Let me offer some comparisons that might help clarify this concept. NASA invests in a great deal of training for astronauts. Why do you think this is the case? Each astronaut comes with a set of abilities and skills already in hand, but the specifics related to making repairs in space, or doing extravehicular activity (EVA, or, as it is more commonly known, a "spacewalk") are not things that come naturally. The astronauts spend hundreds of hours training, pushing themselves through rehearsals of the planned activities, and a set of potential emergency scenarios, until the activities, or behaviors, become instinctive through repetition.

As another example, consider a martial arts expert. Many such experts have natural athletic talent, yet the specific motions and stances necessary to perform their art are anything but instinctive in the beginning. Those who become experts have spent hundreds of hours in the dojo training their bodies to react in very specific ways. They repeat motions, stances, blocks, and strikes so many times that they develop 'muscle memory,' a term used to describe the combination of developing physical strength and agility, as well as mental coordination related to very specific motions. They literally train their minds and bodies to instinctively react in a particular way when faced with certain challenges or threats. What was once totally foreign, is trained to the point of becoming completely instinctive behavior. This acting-without-thinking kind of instinct is referred to a *mushin* in the martial arts.

A Sensei once relayed a story to me in which he was riding an open, construction elevator with a coworker. The coworker was standing beside him and quickly swatted at a bee. From the corner of his eye, the Sensei saw the coworker's hand flying up. He instinctively raised his arm in a blocking motion – without thinking about it. His mind and body had been so trained by years of study, that seeing an arm raising rapidly in the direction of his head triggered an instinctive, protective response. That is instinctive behavior.[92]

Intentional Behavior

This brings us to intentional behavior. These are behaviors that are developed through very intentional efforts. As described above, when we practice a behavior repeatedly, it will eventually become instinctive. In fact, with very few exceptions, such practice is required to create instinct.

There are two key ways in which such a practice can be developed. Either we are forced into situations that require us to practice certain behaviors and we develop strong skills out of pure necessity, or we are intentional about seeking out training, development, and opportunity to practice these behaviors. Both forced and intentional development of capabilities can be extremely valuable, and often the greatest expertise combines the two, such that we are forced to pursue certain skills development, and then intentionally pursue training to further enhance our abilities.

Remember the 'capitalization learning' presented by Malcolm Gladwell. He also describes the concept of 'compensation learning.' This is learning that is forced upon us. We are forced to learn how to do something to

---

[92] Story repeatedly relayed by Sensei Ron Marchetti during advanced training events. Ueshiro Shorin Ryu Karate USA.

survive (either figurative survival or, in some cases, literal survival). Mr. Gladwell describes 'compensation learning' as that which comes out of necessity, rather than natural ability. In other words, when we face challenges in life that require us to learn, adapt, and overcome, we learn in a powerful way. Mr. Gladwell says, "what is learned out of necessity is inevitably more powerful than the learning that comes easily."[93]

While it is true that challenges that force learning upon us are the most powerful means of learning, it is unwise for us to sit idly by, waiting for a challenge to appear that requires learning. Such idleness will likely make us vulnerable to challenge, as opposed to creating an opportunity for 'compensation learning.' Instead, being intentional about learning and developing is the best approach. This will allow us to learn on a constant basis and will provide the best possible equipping for maximizing the potential for learning when challenges occur.

Every challenge is simply an opportunity dressed for work – an opportunity awaiting action. Every failure is a lesson to be learned. Learning from challenges and failure requires intentional, proactive behavior.

Every challenge is an opportunity dressed for work – an opportunity awaiting action.

In order for us to achieve ideal learning and development over time, we want to be intentional, we want to capitalize on our intrinsic abilities, and we want to develop strong instincts.

---

[93] Gladwell. 113.

As leaders, we need to have a breadth of skill. We certainly want to develop our intrinsic abilities to create instinctive behavior, and we want to develop this to the point of expertise.

To be a STAR Leader™, this simply isn't enough. We also need to develop behavioral skills and abilities in areas that do not necessarily come naturally to us. For instance, introverted leaders will need to develop skills in extroversion to improve communication and relationship development. Extroverts will need to develop skills in introversion to improve planning and discernment. We want to maximize the potential for developing expertise in our intrinsic behaviors, and we also need to create instinctive behaviors in areas that don't come to us naturally.

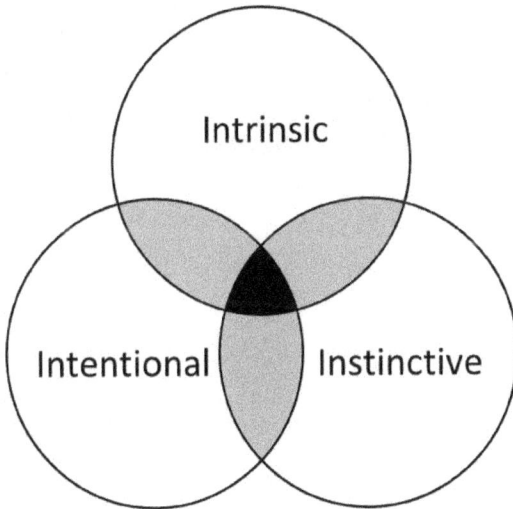

Figure 8. Intrinsic, Intentional, Instinctive Behaviors

As can be seen in the Venn diagram, each of these behavior types may be represented by a circle. Some, but not necessarily all, intrinsic behaviors are instinctive. We may, or may not, be intentional about developing intrinsic behaviors. Some of the behaviors receiving intentional development become instinctive, while others may not. The areas of overlap are where our behaviors will demonstrate the most consistency and highest skill level. The gray overlapping areas will indicate higher than normal skill level. The black area, where all three types of behavior overlap, is where we will develop true expertise.

The goal is to maximize the black area where all three types of behaviors overlap. In other words, maximize your expertise. Ideally, all our intrinsic behaviors, those behaviors based on natural skills and abilities, will receive sufficient intentional development and practice to drive them to become instinctive. This is the maximum possible capitalization on natural skills and abilities that anyone can achieve. This is represented by the diagram below in which the 'Intrinsic' circle is entirely inside the instinctive circle, indicating that every intrinsic behavior has been developed into instinctive behavior.

We will also want to develop instinctive behavior in some areas that do not come as naturally. Therefore, the 'Instinctive' circle is larger than the 'Intrinsic' circle. There are behaviors based on skills that we do not naturally possess, but that we must possess as instinctive behaviors to be successful leaders.

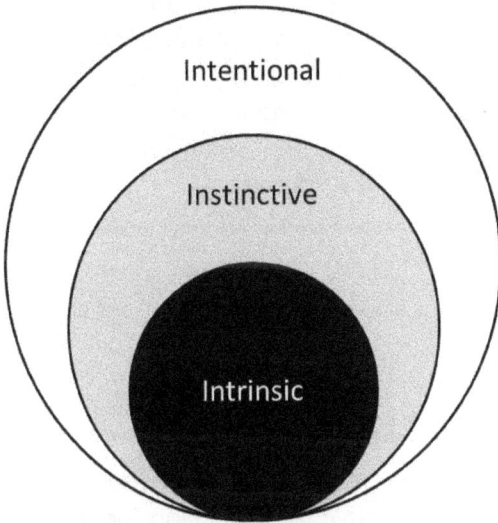

Intentional

Instinctive

Intrinsic

Figure 9. Ideal Relationship Between Intrinsic, Instinctive, and Intentional Behaviors

Finally, all behavior that is necessary for leadership will require intentional skills development. Some of these intentionally developed skills will be intrinsic, yet many will not come so naturally to us. To be STAR Leaders™ that are highly successful at meeting goals and objectives, we will need to intentionally develop some of our skills into instinctive behaviors to become experts in these areas. In other cases, we will need to develop a certain level of skill that is not necessarily at the expert level. These are areas in which we delegate to others who are more skilled than we are. Our own skill level will need to be developed sufficiently to understand what others are doing and to be able to help as needed to ensure successful achievement of objectives. This will require intentional development, just not as much development and practice as is required to develop instinctive expertise.

Nothing in life is ever ideal. Don't be discouraged by this. Our diagram of the relationship between these three types of behaviors will be somewhere in between these two figures. The "intrinsic" circle will not be completely within the "instinctive" circle, yet this should be the ideal for which we strive. The semantics here are important.

Aiming for perfection, and being a little off target, is significantly more valuable than simply aiming for the target and landing somewhere nearby.

We may never achieve "ideal," yet we should always strive for it. Aiming for perfection, and being a little off target, is significantly more valuable than simply aiming for the target and landing somewhere nearby.

Set your standards high and never be content with what you already know. Maintain a teachable attitude that is always searching for something to learn in any given situation. Once again, Mr. Kotter teaches, "...people with high standards and a strong willingness to learn became measurably stronger and more able leaders at age fifty than they had been at age forty."[94]

---

[94] Leading Change. 186.

Set your standards high and never be content with what you already know.

Improving Leadership

To improve our leadership behaviors, we must possess the desire to improve, the humility to understand that we always need to learn, and the attitude of being intentional in learning at every opportunity. We also need the tools to determine what we need to improve and how to accomplish that improvement.

Desire is not something that you can be taught. You must develop that on your own, and I must assume if you read this far in this book you already have the desire to learn. Humility can be cultivated over time. Like desire, it is not something that others can provide for you.

In this section, I'd like to briefly address the key tools needed to improve. You need to be able to assess the current state, create an improvement plan, monitor results over time, and make course corrections to the implementation as needed.

Assessing & Monitoring

Assessing and monitoring your leadership behaviors and the effectiveness with which you are providing leadership requires honest introspection and an openness to feedback. I've combined the ideas of assessment and monitoring because they are very closely related. An assessment is essentially an evaluation of where you stand at a point in time. Monitoring is the act of observing the progress over a period. In other words, a reassessment that evaluates not only where you are now, but how far you've come since the previous assessment. With time, you can begin to establish a trend and get a better idea of what works, and what doesn't.

Whenever possible, I believe that working with an impartial coach to complete the assessments and guide the monitoring is critical. Self-assessments, guided by an impartial coach, are extremely valuable. Ideally, an external coach (e.g. not an employee of the company) should be used to maintain impartiality and openness in conversations. When that isn't possible, a higher-ranking leader, preferably from a different department, should be assigned as a coach to each positional leader within the organizational hierarchy. When I say, 'positional leader', I am referring to those holding an official office with responsibility for the actions of others. In an ideal organization, everyone is a leader, though not everyone holds an official leadership office.

The frequency of such assessment and coaching depends on the individual and the goals to be accomplished. When faced with a need for significant organizational or individual change, monthly assessment and coaching should be considered the minimum. In many cases, a weekly assessment is advised for some initial period, graduated to a monthly program as the change or improvement is being implemented.

As an example, consider the situation of a manufacturing engineer that has seven years of experience working in a production environment. She has performed remarkably as an engineer. She has designed improvements to the production process, implementing changes in procedures to streamline the process and improve efficiency. She has performed work studies to identify bottlenecks and has brought several new production lines and the associated equipment online. In her seventh year, she notes a job posting for a production manager position, applies, and gets the job. Now what? She has proven to be a top-notch engineer, and now holds the responsibility for a production team of 15 people, and the associated processes and equipment. Although a proven leader among her engineering peers, she has no formal experience in leadership roles. While she knows how to perform work studies and improve process efficiencies, she has little experience or training on how to effectively influence those on her team to perform at their best.

I see this all the time. People excel in technical roles – engineers, accountants, technicians, nurses, doctors, etc. – but fail when promoted to supervisory roles. What frustrates me is that those who place these technical geniuses in supervisor roles respond to their failure with attitudes like, "Well, we gave her a shot. I guess she's just not cut out for leadership." But the truth of the matter is, she was set up to fail. They didn't give her a shot; they simply piled on responsibility with no guidance on how to deliver on that responsibility. The real failure is on the ones who failed to provide the coaching needed for her to succeed.

Every time you try something new – like transitioning from a technical role to a supervisory role – you will experience failure. It's part of the learning process. When those going through such transitions are provided with proper training and coaching, the magnitude and frequency of failures will be significantly reduced.

More importantly, the learning process will happen at a much faster pace as coaching provides not only basic guidance but also assistance in how to learn from mistakes and failures.

For the leader, there are several areas of assessment that I believe are critical. Start with the basics by assessing personality and the pillars of leadership. Next, assess leadership practices and key proficiency skills. It may also be helpful to consider assessing how you approach leadership, and the direction of focus for your efforts to influence others, the leadership styles that come most naturally to you (and those which need more work), and your development level in areas of importance to your specific role.

Personality

Personality tests are often utilized as a means of determining one's potential to lead. This is a huge mistake! Those who use tests such as these in this manner will approach the process with preconceived notions about what personality traits are required of great leaders. If this is your approach, I suggest you read *Strategic Leadership* where I describe the value of different personality traits in leadership, and how different characteristics may be ideal in different scenarios. This is a hold-over of the old Trait Theory. Even though Trait Theory has been proven to be incorrect in study after study, it still remains a persistent assumption among many in leadership roles. Personality type is NOT an indicator of leadership potential. It just isn't.

If you still aren't convinced, spend a few minutes reviewing the characteristics exemplified by each personality type in the

Meyers-Brigg Type Indicator (MBTI). You can find these descriptions online with a simple web search on MBTI descriptions. Pick one of the sixteen types that you think would make the ideal leader. Compare that to the personality types of the Presidents of the United States. (Search online; you'll find several listings). Better yet, list whom you believe are the top five Presidents in U.S. history and compare your selected 'ideal personality' with your 'top five' list. How many of these top five have the personality you selected as ideal for leaders? In fact, of the five best you selected, how many different personality types are represented?

If I were to answer that question, the five top Presidents of the U.S. that I would pick represent five different personality types. To avoid clouding the intended lessons on leadership with political opinion and ideology, I'm not going to list whom my selections are; however, I will tell you some facts about their personalities.

Having used multiple sources of estimates for Presidential personalities, there is a great deal of consistency between the estimates; however, they are not all perfectly identical.[95] When looking at the top five, the total in each type should be viewed as +/- 0.5 (e.g. 2 out of 5 is really 1.5-2.5 out of 5, and 3 out of 5 is really 2.5-3.5 out of 5; therefore, 2 or 3 out of 5 should really be considered equivalent). When considering all 44 U.S. Presidents, the margin of error (e.g. the variation between estimates) is less than 5%. So, for the sake of being

---

[95] Based on numerous online sources reviewed and 'averaged' to estimate the personality types. There is strong correlation between different estimates found but still some variation (on the order of +/- 1 out of 5 for the top 5 ranking, so that a 2/3 split should be considered even).

conservative, let's assume 5%. For instance, 3 out of the top 5 Presidents are estimated to be introverts; this should be considered an even split between introverts and extroverts. When looking at the entire population, 57% of the U.S. Presidents were introverts.[96] It may be surprising that Presidential personality types lean slightly more toward introversion than extraversion, yet the difference is small when considering the possible margin of error (57%±5%).[97,98]

Table 3. Presidential Personalities

I/E	S/N	T/F	J/P
57% introvert 43% extrovert	40% sensing 60% intuition	80% thinking 20% feeling	40% judging 60% perceiving

Sensing vs. intuition, and judging vs. perceiving, were similarly split – very close, but slightly leaning towards intuition and perceiving. When looking at the thinking vs. feeling type, the total population of presidents indicates 80% exhibited the thinking type, as opposed to the feeling type. Narrowing the list down to my personal top five picks didn't change this ratio. Four out of my top five were thinking. However, keep in mind that this doesn't necessarily mean thinking is more advantageous than feeling. There are times when the feeling type will have the advantage. The one President with the feeling type in my top five is still in that top five

---

[96] "Personality Types of All U.S. Presidents (Chronological)." *The Sixteen Types*. Web. 20 Feb 2018.

[97] Jensen III, Lorenzo. "What Every President Would Have Scored on the Myers-Briggs Test." *Though Catalog*. Web 20 Feb 2018.

[98] Speer, Jack. "Personality Type & Presidents." *World Type Alliance*. Web 20 Feb 2018.

list – he'd probably still be on my list if it were narrowed to the top three. He skillfully utilized this aspect of his personality to lead the nation and surrounded himself with staff that were strong in the thinking type.

Simply put, personality is not an indicator of leadership potential. Personality assessments have great value when appropriately utilized. However, they are inappropriate for determining one's potential to lead – even though they are often used for this purpose. Loyalty, determination, perseverance, and vision are far more important to one's ability to lead, and each of these critical characteristics can be exhibited by any personality type.

While they cannot indicate an individual's ability to lead, personality assessments can identify strengths and weaknesses. Each personality type has a natural strength in certain areas that are important to leadership, and a need to work more on developing other areas.

Assessing your personality type, and that of those you work with is also helpful in identifying how people communicate (and thus can help you improve your own communication).

There are many tools widely available for personality assessment. No tool is perfect. Each has its own set of strengths and weaknesses, yet most of them will provide you with beneficial information. It is not the purpose of this book to provide a personality assessment tool. Rather, the intent is to discuss the advantages of using the tools that are available in a positive and productive manner.

When hired to assess leaders, many coaches have them undergo a battery of personality tests to establish a baseline of their strengths and weakness. Once the results are received, they discuss the results and then determine how they may be useful to generate intentional action. I would suggest using a variety of tools and reap the benefits of each. Some reliable ones are the Meyers-Brigg Type Indicator® (MBTI®)[99] which was used for the previous Presidential personality example, the Personal Style Inventory[100], and the DiSC®[101] assessment.

Pillars

The Pillars of STAR Leadership™ are what I consider to be the foundation of leadership. This doesn't necessarily mean that all leaders possess these characteristics; however, I do believe that for a STAR Leader™ that contributes positively to society, these characteristics, or pillars, are foundationally essential: character, courage, confidence, communication, culture, competence, and coaching. We discussed these pillars at length in *Strategic Leadership*, so I won't repeat that message here. However, I do want to provide a summary while highlighting that these seven C's are cultivated over time and can be developed and improved with intentional action.

Character defines what a leader will do when no one is looking. It is the core integrity

---

[99] Myers-Brigg Type Indicator and MBTI are registered trademarks of The Myers & Briggs Foundation (2014).
[100] Copyright©1979 by D.W. Champagne and R.C. Hogan
[101] "DiSC is a behavior assessment tool based on the DISC theory of psychologist William Moulton Marston, which centers on four different behavioral traits: dominance, inducement, submission, and compliance. This theory was then developed into a behavioral assessment tool by industrial psychologist Walter Vernon Clarke." ("William Moulton Marston". *Wikipedia*. Web. 26 September 2016.) DiSC® is a registered trademark of John Wiley & Sons, Inc.

of the person. One isn't born with character. Anyone with a two-year-old knows that to be true. Character is developed through disciplined practice. You cannot develop character by chance. You must cultivate it and anchor it in your life.

Courage is built on the foundation of inspiration. When inspired by a passionate vision, people will surprise you with the courage that they demonstrate. Courage is very difficult to muster when a vision is missing or uninspiring. But, when a vision captures the hearts of people, courage will flow naturally. Courage is also related to character. In general, the stronger a person's character, the greater the courage that they demonstrate in the face of adversity.

Confidence is essential to moving forward, and getting things done. One cannot lead without confidence in the vision, in the team, in individuals, and in oneself.

Communication is required to build and sustain a team. Communication shares information, tears down walls, builds bridges, provides instruction, and collects data. In a military operation, one of the first targets is the enemy's communication infrastructure. Destroy their ability to communicate and you weaken their ability to work together, thus drastically reducing their effectiveness. Don't let this happen to your team. Prioritize strong communication that empowers effective teamwork.

Culture is the essential behaviors of the organization, and it rests squarely on the leader's shoulders. Leadership sets the tone for these behaviors, so the leader must set the example for the organization to follow.

Competence simply means an ability to get things done. Leaders must have competence in team-building and in the specific areas of responsibility that define their organization.

Coaching is something every leader must do. Having a heart to coach others is necessary to cultivate a team that is constantly improving and taking on new challenges.

Assessing an individual's strengths and weaknesses in these pillars can be difficult. It requires the individual to be totally honest to receive sound feedback. When doing this assessment, I like to have the individual do a self-assessment, while selecting several colleagues to perform a 360° review as well. By selectively choosing anonymous reviews that are direct reports, some that are at the same level of authority, and, if possible, some that rank above the individual in the organizational hierarchy, we can create a picture of how others view the individual.

I have developed a test that asks the individual to respond to thirty-five questions related to the Seven Pillars of STAR Leadership™. The results are then tabulated to provide a graph of each of the seven pillars. This graph can be used to provide an estimated snapshot of the current state of each of the pillars for the individual.

If something is way off (e.g. they score very low in one or more of these pillars of leadership), this test may be used to validate one's acceptability as a leader in your organization. In other words, you, as the leader, must decide which pillars you can train and which pillars are essential for an individual to score highly on prior to joining your team. For instance, if someone scored a 5-10, out of 25, on character, you may want to reconsider whether this person is a good match for your team. If a person is dishonest or untrustworthy, this is unlikely to be improved with any amount of training. On the other hand, they may have a lower than desired score in competency because they are new to a particular role. Some training and coaching will allow them to improve this score.

However, test scores such as these are generally best used to help leaders, or potential leaders, identify those areas in which they need the most improvement. This will help guide them in the creation of a personal development plan. For instance, those who score low on communication may need to pursue some training to improve those skills; they need to be intentional about putting themselves in positions that require them to communicate effectively.

Consider the radial chart (Figure 10) provided as an example of the results of the Seven Pillars Test. The chart of a perfect, ideal leader would be completely solid so that none of the lighter circumferential grid lines would be visible.

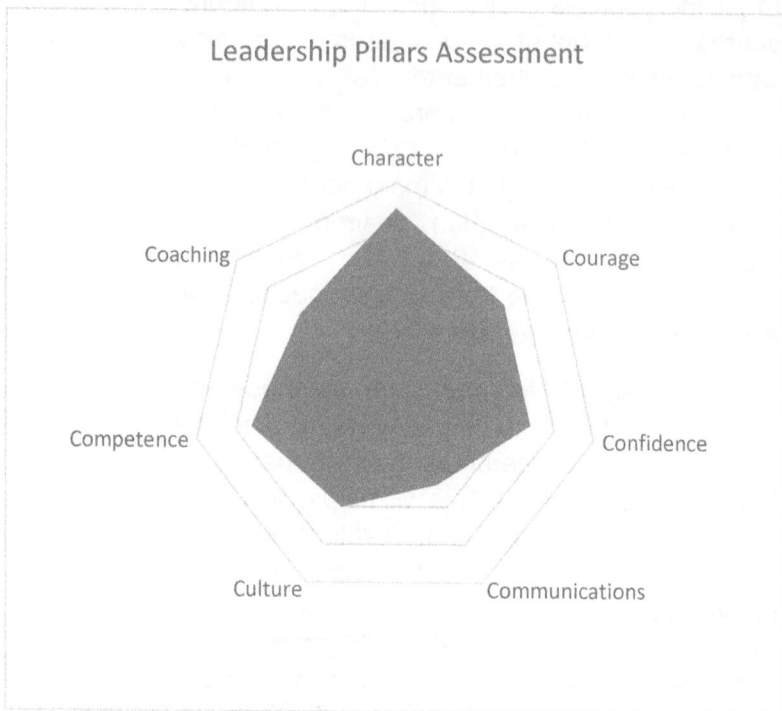

Figure 10. Sample Leadership Pillars Assessment Results

This hypothetical individual scored well on character, and satisfactory on competence, confidence, and courage. Intuitively, we can see how the apparent relationship between competence, confidence, and courage makes sense. However, pillars don't always match up so perfectly. This individual's skill at coaching and culture-building leave much room for improvement, whereas communications skills need immediate attention.

This individual should be praised for character and encouraged to persevere through challenges in that area that may be presented in the near future.

As a priority, I would also discuss the low communications score. Using questions to guide the conversation, my intent is to get to the root-cause behind this score. What specific issues or concerns need to be addressed? A 360° assessment, along with a comparison between the individual's self-assessment and that of the larger group, can often help identify areas most in need of improvement. I often find that individuals are more critical of themselves than the group will be; however, it isn't uncommon for there to be at least one pillar in which individuals scored themselves much higher than the group. Sometimes, we just cannot see the problem when we are viewing it from within our own perspectives.

Finally, the process of deeper investigation on other areas needing improvement is repeated. This would be done in order of priority – lowest scoring pillars are addressed first. In the end, we have a detailed report of areas that individuals need to improve to solidify their foundation in leadership.

The frequency with which this assessment is performed is dependent upon the need for improvement. If there are several pillars in need of significant improvement, it might be worthwhile to re-assess on a quarterly basis, or even a monthly basis, in extreme cases. Typically, I would recommend an annual re-assessment to determine how well the development plan has been executed and to make any needed adjustments to the plan for the following year.

As described earlier in this book, there are seven key practices in which every leader must engage on a routine basis. No one will perfect every practice. Some practices will come more naturally to you, while with others you will struggle. Recall that these practices include being a champion of purpose and principles, intentionally cultivating the Vision Vector™, proactively modeling the mojo, coaching performance, building unity on your team without promoting uniformity, enabling and empowering, and focusing the operation.

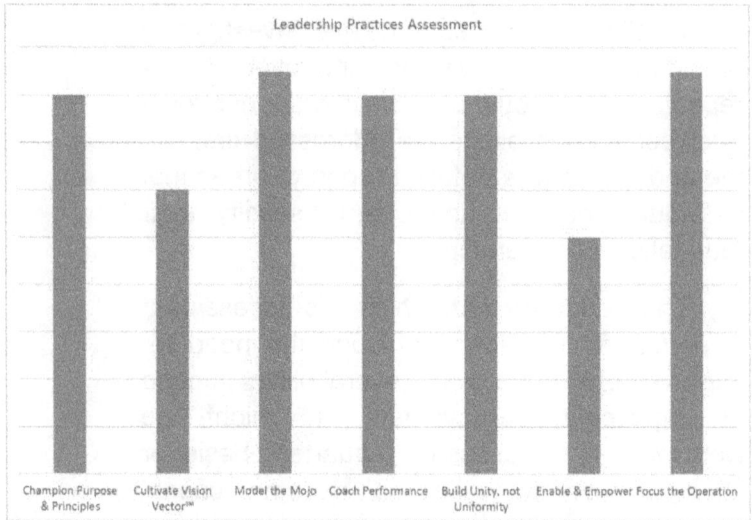

Figure 11. Sample Leadership Practices Assessment Results

In this case, I've provided a bar chart (Figure 11) as a sample of the results of an assessment, another way to view the same data. From the chart, you can see that this individual has the greatest strength in modeling the mojo and focusing the operation. This individual remains strong in championing purpose and principles, coaching performance, and building unity. However, this person isn't effectively cultivating the Vision Vector™ and needs a great deal of improvement in the ability to enable and empower members of the team.

A full 360° assessment of the leadership practices should be performed annually. I would also recommend performing the self-assessment on a quarterly basis, employing the help of a good coach to guide the process of comparing the results to the development plan and making any needed course corrections. In some cases, such as in areas in need of urgent improvement, this should be done monthly.

This data can also be displayed in a radial plot, as was shown for the Pillars of Leadership© example. This chart is excellent for the frequent spot checks because it is a simple and effective visual cue. The more circular the plot appears, the more balanced the individual is. Of course, the plot is a seven-sided polygon, so it will never be perfectly circular. Imagine a curved line connecting each point rather than a straight line. If all the points were scored perfectly, this curved line would form a perfect circle. However, when one of the practices is lagging, it creates an out-of-round image, making it obvious where attention is needed.

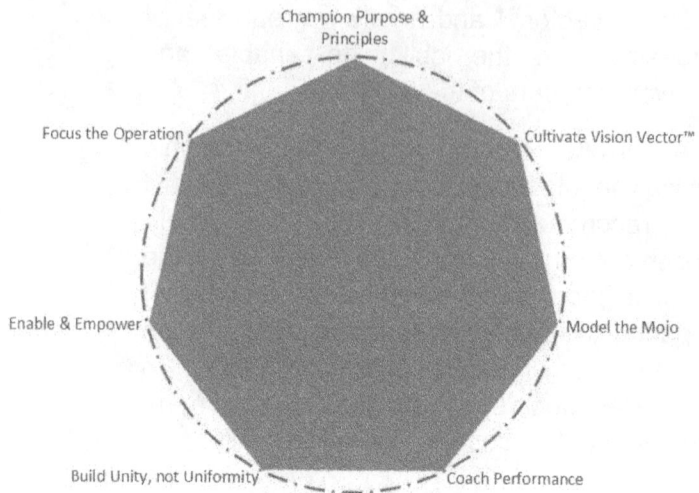

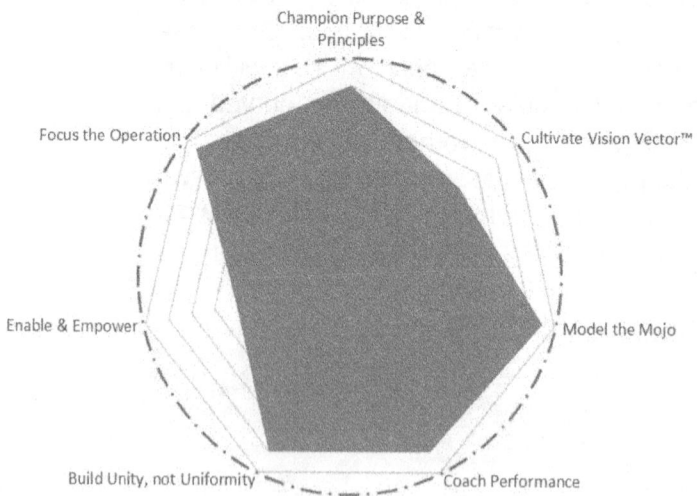

Figure 12. Comparison between well-balanced and out-of-balance leadership practice wheels

Proficiency

In addition to the everyday practices that are essential to STAR Leadership, there are several skills that great leaders must possess: operations skills, people skills, and strategic thinking skills. For each of the above categories, I've included a summary of five key skills that I believe are critical to great leadership. This is, by no means, an exhaustive list of leadership skills, yet I believe that measuring and developing skill level in each of these areas will greatly enhance one's ability to lead effectively.

Operations skills include a proficiency in general administration of the operations, technical competence in the areas of critical importance to the specific role or organization, sound time management, decisiveness, and intelligent goal setting.

People skills include a proficiency in communication, listening, peacemaking, the ability to adapt to specific situations, and the ability to coach and mentor others.

Strategic skills involve proficiency in critical thinking, discernment with limited information at hand, initiative, grit or 'stickiness,' and a personal commitment to lifelong learning.

Any given leader will be naturally strong in one category and weak in another. Maintaining proficiency in all three categories of skills will require intentional activity. The areas of weakness can be strengthened by learning and developing new skills. All skill areas will require proactive practice to fine tune.

Leadership Skills

Operational Skills
Administration
Technical Competence
Time Management
Decisiveness
Goal Setting

People Skills
Communication
Listening
Peacemaking
Adaptability
Coaching

Strategic Skills
Critical Thinking
Discernment
Initiative
Grit
Lifelong Learning

Administration

Administration is the ability to perform the duties of managing the operations of an organization. This skill is a conglomeration, or set, of specific skills, which may vary from one organization to the next depending upon the leadership role and the requirements of that role. In the most general terms, a leader must be skilled in the areas necessary to sustain the operations at a high-performance level.

At high levels of leadership, this will often require some skill in financial management, business process management, sales management, and other critical functions. This does not necessarily mean that the leader must be an expert in each of these areas; however, the leader will need to have proficiency in each area to allow for intelligent conversations and questioning of the experts.

For instance, it isn't necessarily required that a CEO be an expert accountant. Yet CEOs must be proficient in financial management in order to understand financial statements and their implications to business operations. CEOs must also be able to ask the executive team pertinent questions. They must be able to tie financial performance with operational performance and keep both areas heavily focused on the strategy.

Competence
Technical competence is also required of leaders. There is no universal set of requirements that will apply to every leader. Head nurses must possess strong technical competence in nursing, lead software programmers must be skilled in writing code, school superintendents must have skill in curriculum development, and attorney partners must be skilled in the law pertaining to their area of expertise, etc.

To evaluate one's level of technical competence, you'll first need to identify the technical skills in which one must be competent.

Time Management

Managing one's time is often overlooked as an essential skill of leadership. Time management requires knowing what is important, and what is not. It requires keeping a calendar and sticking to the schedule.

Outside help to maintain this skill is common. Many great leaders have so many things going on simultaneously that they can't keep track of every task and meeting. So, they delegate this task by hiring executive assistants that are superb time managers.

Decisiveness

Being decisive means possessing the ability to make swift and reliable decisions to settle an issue or produce a definite result. Leadership requires the skill of gathering information available from multiple sources and then making decisions quickly.

The sources of information aiding in the decision-making process may include operational data collection, input from team members, input from external sources, personal observations, and even gut feelings. Great leadership requires an ability to make swift decisions, get the team on board with implementing the decisions, and following up to ensure proper execution of the decisions.

Great leadership will also require a strong grasp of the criticality of the decision to be made, as well as balancing this criticality with the ability to collect additional information to reduce risk. For instance, during a rescue operation, a fireman must assess the situation quickly and decide which is the safest exit route. He may rely on his own observations of the structure, and on information about the nature of the fire relayed to him over the radio. The situation is critical because any delay in decision-making could be catastrophic. The fireman rapidly processes available information and informs others of his decision as he rescues victims and begins his exit. An example of a less critical decision might be deciding what type of food to serve at the next staff meeting, which allows the decision-maker the time to survey the participants to determine preferences.

Being decisive balances taking the time necessary to make good decisions with avoiding unnecessary delays in the decision-making process. Decisions should be made as quickly as possible to minimize risk and maximize the probability of a desirable outcome.

Goal Setting

Setting goals is another important operational skill that leaders must possess. Goal-setting can range from the daily 'to-do list' to larger program goals and milestones. It certainly includes the 'big picture,' strategic objectives, as well as what you need to accomplish today, this week, this month, and so on.

Leaders must be able to set goals for themselves. This is a foundational requirement. Great leaders know how to set goals for those that they lead. Helping others develop and reach goals is an essential part of leadership.

Communication

The ability to gain information, to convey information, to provide instructions, to clarify goals and expectations, and to influence others requires a strong ability to communicate. If you can't communicate, you won't be able to effectively lead.

Communication is one of the pillars of leadership, and it is also a critical skill. Being a good communicator requires adaptability and an understanding of how people absorb information. We focused on this concept in the prior section on learning and communication styles. It is a key part of the leadership process.

Listening

Listening is part of the communication process and is a distinct and important skill. When you speak, you are sharing what you know with others. When you listen, you are seeking to increase your knowledge by absorbing knowledge from others.

The knowledge gained by listening may be related to the operations of your organization. It may be related to the team, or to the individual. It may be related to any number of external factors, or it may be related to you. The truth is, you can't learn and develop without listening to what others have to say. You also can't understand the perspective of others on your team without listening to them. An ability to listen is much more than simply an ability to remain quiet while others talk. It requires the use of questions and the ability to focus on the details of what is being said in order to acquire knowledge that you didn't previously have.

Listening is essential to accepting reproof. Even the greatest leader is imperfect and will make mistakes. What separates those that sustain great leadership from those that don't is a willingness to listen when confronted with truth.

This doesn't mean the leader allows disrespect. Rather, it means the leader eagerly listens when respectful admonishment is given. When your team fears presenting truth to you because of the reaction they expect, you are no longer receiving the truth you need to perform at your best.

When your team fears presenting truth to you because of the reaction they expect, you are no longer receiving the truth you need to perform at your best.

"Like a gold ring or an ornament of gold is a wise reprover to a listening ear" (Proverbs 25:12)[102]. As a leader, you may need to be a wise reprover on one occasion, and a listening ear on another. For "the ear that listens to life-giving reproof will dwell among the wise. Whoever ignores instruction despises himself, but he who listens to reproof gains intelligence" (Proverbs 15:31-32)[103].

Listening also conveys importance. When you listen to someone, you are telling them they are important enough to sacrifice a portion of your time to hear and process what they have to say. This is of tremendous importance to leadership. If people don't believe you find them, and what they have to say, to be important, then they are less likely to be influenced by what you do and say.

Peacemaking
A 'peacemaker' is one who works to establish peace between those who disagree or are in conflict. For the leader, peacemaking is

---

[102] *The Bible*. English Standard Version. Crossway, 2001.
[103] *The Bible*. English Standard Version. Crossway, 2001.

the ability to resolve conflicts among the team. In the first century, the Apostle Paul provided great wisdom on this topic when he said, "If possible, so far as it depends on you, live peaceably with all" (Romans 12:18)[104].

Anytime you involve two or more people working together towards common goals, conflict is inevitable. Conflicts will occur due to clashing approaches, personality differences, priority differences, and the like. The team will consist of dedicated, yet imperfect individuals. These imperfections will always produce conflicts at some level.

The leader's responsibility is to recognize the difference between healthy conflict, which helps a team arrive at the best solution, and unhealthy conflict, which drives a wedge between people and inhibits peak performance. Simultaneously balancing healthy conflict with keeping the peace is necessary for great leadership.

Those in conflict have a choice in how to respond. These choices are flight, fight, or fix.

- *Flight* is the escape response. This response includes burying your head in the sand and pretending the conflict doesn't exist, throwing gas on the fire by blaming someone else for the conflict (and thus avoiding the part we play in the process), or simply running away and avoiding the conflict. While we may avoid the problem temporarily, none of these responses solves the problem. In each of these cases, the root cause of

---

[104] *The Bible.* English Standard Version. Crossway, 2001.

the problems remains, bubbling just beneath the surface, and will eventually blow up into a much larger problem.

- *Fight* is the response that involves attacks on others involved. These attacks may be in the form of gossip, insults and verbal cruelty, trash-talking, or even physical force. Those who respond with a fight may get their way, but they will lose the respect of others and diminish the effectiveness of the team.

- *Fix* the problem is the response in which the parties involved take the time to work out their problems. This will often require forgiveness and will always require communication. To work out a conflict, the root causes must be discussed, perspectives need to be considered and understood, and ideas must be listened to and valued. It takes strong leadership to keep this on track.

As the leader, you must be diligent about avoiding the fight or flight responses. You must guide your team through the steps necessary to fix the problem that is the basis for the conflict. Only then will you avoid unhealthy conflicts that reduce team efficiency and effectiveness.

Let me share an example. Years ago, I was managing a product development team. My office happened to be located within earshot of the production floor so that I could hear what was going on when debates occurred. I witnessed a conflict occurring between two people on the production floor. It began as a healthy conflict over how to properly perform a quality test on the product that they were assembling but quickly turned unfriendly with aggressively loud, personal insults being slung back and forth. Their supervisor was out of the office at the time, so this confrontation was heating up without any reasonable constraint.

I stepped into the room where this conflict was occurring, and immediately said each of their names in a stern and commanding tone and instructed them to meet me in my office right away. I gave them a brief lecture on the importance of teamwork and the requirement to disagree respectfully. Then I told them to go home for a few hours and return to meet individually with me later in the afternoon. When I later met with each of them individually, I asked them to share their side of the story, listening intently to their grievances. I was careful not to make light of their feelings of being mistreated yet, using questions as a tool to open their eyes, guided them to see how their method of communication was ineffective and just made matters worse.

Finally, I had asked both of them to meet me in my office. I asked them to listen to what I was about to say, just as I had listened to each them. I discussed the major points of each of their concerns and described how they could have handled the situation better. I then asked them, one at a time, if they would like to restate their concerns to the other in a civilized and respectful manner. Each of them did, however, their list of grievances was much shorter by this time. Listening to me describe their concerns in front of the other allowed them to see how petty and insignificant most of their grievances really were. After airing their concerns, the two shook hands and then began discussing the pros and cons of the two approaches to solving the problem that led to the conflict in the first place.

I could have ignored the conflict – after all, they weren't my direct reports. I could have simply fired them both on the spot. I could have joined the screaming match myself. None of this would have accomplished anything. Instead, by playing the role of peacemaker, the team relationships were restored. These two probably never became 'best buds'. But they did develop an ability to work together and discuss their differences without resorting to shouting matches.

Adaptability

Adaptability is key. Always keep in mind the level of experience of those whom you are leading and the learning and communication style you believe will work best. In addition, be flexible regarding the priority and risk tolerance of the task in question as well as other variables that may affect the mission.

Your ability to adapt effectively will be driven by your ability to recognize the needs of the situation, your mastery of the styles and behaviors available to you, and the fluidity with which you are able to jump from one style to the next.

You won't become an expert overnight. It takes time and intentional practice to develop adaptability. You will need to continually educate yourself, intentionally apply what you learn through practice, and proactively integrate these new skills into your natural routine by making them habitual and by mentoring them for others. Part of mentoring others is leading by example, and part of it is teaching others to practice the same leadership skills. In my practice of karate, having someone show me a new kata gives me a nice introduction to it, taking time to practice it myself allows me to learn it well, and teaching it to someone else encourages a deeper understanding that leads to expertise. As you read this book, you are being introduced to the principles it contains – including adaptability. Reading is a great start, but it only brings you value when you put the principles into practice. And if you want to really develop expertise in these principles you'll have to teach them to others.

Coaching

Coaching is a pillar of STAR Leadership™. It involves encouraging, empowering, and enabling those that you lead.

To be a great leader, you must freely provide encouragement. But, you must first learn to recognize the signals that people give when they need encouragement. Often, people don't realize that they are giving such signals. Signals such as a discouraged spirit, self-deprecating (or team-deprecating) language, stooping posture, slow performance, and the like will provide an indication that encouragement is needed.

Some time ago, I was charged with leading a product development team. I made a habit of walking through the lab daily and checking in with each team member. Sometimes I asked for a quick status update on a project, but generally, my visit just involved a 'good morning' or 'how was your weekend' type of chat. I distinctly recall one situation where nearly everyone I spoke to seemed to be having a rough day. And, it was still early in the morning! The down-and-out attitudes were permeating the team and killing productivity.

A few minutes later, I returned to let everyone know we were going to have a mandatory team meeting in the conference room before lunch. I'm sure there was a lot of discussion about why we were having that meeting. When the meeting began, I thanked each one of the team for their hard work, told them I was proud of them, then took them all to a local ice cream shop for a treat. I also made it clear that this was a paid meeting rather than an unpaid lunch break (which was particularly important for the hourly team members).

They were shocked at first and didn't know what to say. But, once we all sat down with our ice cream, everyone's mood changed. They were openly conversing and laughing. The stresses they all had experienced that morning seemed to melt away almost as fast as the ice cream on that hot, summer day.

Later in the day, I made another pass through the lab to see how everyone was doing. The laughter and open conversation had continued. Everyone was diligently working, and noticeable progress was being made. Their attitudes had shifted, and teamwork was prevailing. Did the ice cream do that? Maybe. Even more so, the team felt valued because their efforts were recognized and appreciated. When people know that someone cares enough to recognize them and reassure them that they can get the job done, attitudes change for the better. Whether we want to admit it or not, we all need this kind of encouragement from time to time.

As previously described in this book, enabling and empowering those that we lead are critical practices of leadership. Successfully implementing these practices will require skill. The leader needs to be skilled at identifying needs and finding ways to meet those needs. The leader must also be good at delegating and mentoring others, to help them develop the competencies needed to carry a growing portion of the load. At times, the leader must coach others by teaching them, and by directing their steps to ensure that the tasks are completed; thus, the team learns during the process.

Critical Thinking

The skill of critical thinking is the ability to objectively analyze a situation or issue and form a judgment. Critical thinking has been described as "a complex process which involves a wide range of skills and attitudes."[105] I'd like to simplify the concept of critical thinking with the definition of the following four-step process: [1] conceptualize, [2] inquire, [3] assess, and [4] judge.

The first step in the critical thinking process is to conceptualize the problem or issue. This involves rational consideration of your own perceptions, as well as a methodical, open-minded compilation of other perspectives and positions – particularly competing views.

The second step is inquiring to gain information. You'll want to know what information was used to formulate each perspective being considered, how this information was collected, and if the information is reliable and valid. This body of information provides the basis of evidence in support of

---

[105] Cottrell, Stella. (2011). *Critical Thinking Skills*, Second Edition. NY: Palgrave Macmillan. 2.

alternative perspectives, and thus the details about the information itself, and the sources used to collect the information. Anything you can learn about the quality and reliability of the information is important.

The use of Socratic questioning is a useful tool to acquire a deeper understanding. Such questioning can be used to:

- Clarify a situation (e.g. clearly state what the situation really is)

- Probe deeper into the assumptions being made (e.g. ask questions about the assumptions that bring them to the surface and challenge their validity or applicability to the situations)

- Determine the reasons and evidence used (e.g. what data is being used to justify the perspective)

- Challenge the viewpoints and perspectives

- Uncover the implications and consequences of the perspective

- Question the question being asked itself.[106]

The third step is the assessment. Obviously, there is overlap between the steps because the questions being asked are also being used to assess the information as it is revealed. The point of assessment is to

---

[106] Thompson, Justin. (2016). *Strategic Leadership*. Viera: 2Xalt Press. 75-76.

determine what the information means and to validate (or invalidate) the information available. It requires the ability to clearly identify false assumptions and to logically review the available information in order to draw clear and actionable conclusions about the arguments presented.

To properly assess information and evidence, you must demonstrate a certain level of skepticism.[107] This doesn't mean you rudely deny all ideas presented. That would be counter-productive. Instead, it means that you politely question every idea and every piece of evidence used to formulate and defend the idea and that you maintain an open mind regarding your own ideas. Keep in mind that this open-mindedness doesn't mean you don't hold fast to important convictions and principles. It does, however, mean that you have carefully thought about your convictions and that you can quickly and easily communicate the evidence for those convictions.

Finally, the point of critical thinking is to arrive at a judgment of the situation. This is the point of the process. Ideally, we will subconsciously put the critical thinking process into action. When critical thinking becomes our natural response to problems and arguments, we know we have truly mastered the skill.

To master the process of critical thinking, we will also need to develop skills in several supporting areas: observation, reasoning, decision-making, analysis, judgment, and persuasion.[108] When you master these skills and persistently apply them to the critical thinking

---

[107] Cottrell. 2.
[108] Cottrell. 4.

process, your ability to influence others will increase. In addition, the precision and accuracy of the action taken because of your influence will be enhanced. That's what great leadership does.

Discernment

Discernment is the ability to judge a situation accurately – to decide between truth and error or between right and wrong. It is closely related to critical thinking. In fact, critical thinking is often the best process through which we achieve discernment. We gain good discernment through experience. Namely, a strong knowledge and familiarity with the foundational elements of the situation is a must. At times, this knowledge and familiarity can only be developed through the intentional application of the critical thinking process. In other cases, the foundational elements are your purpose, principles, passion, and persistence.

Discernment is possible when your purpose and principles are clearly defined, well understood, and passionately close to your heart. When opportunities arise, you will then be able to quickly recognize their alignment with your purpose and principles, and how (or if) they contribute to your vision. A discerning mind will avoid those opportunities that either contradict your purpose and principles, or distract from your vision.

Initiative

Initiative is the proactive nature of jumping in to act or take charge before others. A leader must take initiative. A leader is the first to act, the first to take charge of a situation, and the first to sacrifice to accomplish an objective. Leaders will sometimes need to push, but they must spend far more time pulling. Pushing is done from behind. A leader that only pushes is likely unwilling to be the first to act. Pulling is done from the front of the line by those who don't hesitate to get in the mud and get dirty to make progress towards goals.

A great leader must always be prepared to act first and pull others with him/her. If you are always waiting on someone else to take the first steps, you are not a leader. Leaders jump into action and pull others to follow their example. Still, there are times when developing those you are leading requires that you give a little push. At such times, a great leader will need to intentionally step back and give people a little push to do more than they thought possible.

Grit/Stickiness

Grit, or stickiness, is your ability to stick with a program through the challenges. The old proverb, "When the going gets tough, the tough get going," sums it up nicely. When problems arise and challenges are revealed, those who have strength of character will get to work and stick with the effort. Another well-known maxim states, "What lies behind us and what lies before us are tiny matters compared to what lies within us."[109]

Learning

We typically think of learning as a means of developing skill rather than a skill in and of itself. The art and science of learning is a powerful and important skill. It takes skill to identify areas in need of development, and additional skill to

---

[109] Unknown. *Meditations in Wall Street*. NY: William Morrow & Co.

intentionally develop a plan for learning what you need to learn to improve.

Learning isn't a one-time event or even a phase. To be a great leader, you must always have a learning mindset. To learn, you must be both observant and teachable. If you lack the ability to observe what is happening around you, learning new things will be a struggle. Similarly, if you are bull-headed and unteachable, you won't learn new things − even if you are observant enough to recognize them. A rather famous proverb by an unknown author states, "If you are not willing to learn, no one can help you. If you are determined to learn, no one can stop you."

Determine to learn.

Be unstoppable.

Each of these leadership skills are intertwined to form a composite structure, one in which multiple materials are woven together to make the structure significantly stronger than the materials would be on their own. For instance, polymer resin forms a strong plastic that is flexible. Thin strands of glass are very strong in tension but break easily when bent at high angles. Combining the two, by suspending the strands of glass within the polymer resin, will produce an extremely strong composite material commonly known as fiberglass. This composite material is used in sports car bodies, boat hulls, and many other structures where light weight, flexibility, and strength are all important.

Like composite materials, the proficiency of leadership is a composite of operations skills, people skills, and strategic skills. Each of these skills is individually important, and, when properly woven together, they produce a powerful composite skill that will enhance the proficiency of leadership.

As with personality, pillars, and practices, the assessment of the skills that determine the proficiency of a leader is important. This assessment should be conducted on an annual basis with development plans created and revised with each assessment. Progress on the development plans can be monitored with the balance wheel tool for leadership proficiency that asks the evaluator to quickly rank the individual in each of the skills noted. It is often beneficial to have this balance wheel ranking done as both a self-assessment and as an independent assessment, in order to compare perspectives on progress. You may identify differences in perspective that will help you fine-tune your development plan and improve results.

Acknowledgments

I would like to thank my wife, Tanya, and kids, Joshua and Hannah, for their patience and encouragement as I've spent many hours preparing this text and the related course materials. Most importantly, I would like to thank the Father, Son, and Holy Spirit who have shown me the meaning of life. To some, this statement will make perfect sense, and to others, it will seem strange and foreign. The concepts of this text are powerful and applicable to your leadership ability regardless of your understanding or agreement with my relationship with God yet let me briefly explain how God has provided meaning.

In the beginning, God created mankind to resemble His own character, to represent His presence on earth, and to have a relationship with Him. This is our purpose. He tells us this in the first chapter of Genesis, which is the first book of His scriptures. He also tells us that our own sin – rejection of His instructions and directions for our lives – has destroyed our ability to live up to the purpose for which He created us. Because of sin – and we are all guilty of sin – none of us has the capacity to resemble His character, to represent Him, or even to have a relationship with Him – instead, we are condemned to an eternal death.

While this seems hopeless, up to this point, God provided hope in the form of His own Son who came to live as a man, die as a sacrifice for the sins of mankind, and rise from the dead to conquer death once and for all who would believe in Him. To some who misunderstand, this may seem elitist because belief in the Son, Jesus Christ, is the only way to restore our ability to resemble His character, represent Him on earth, and live in relationship with Him now and forever. Once we understand that we are condemned because of our sin, and yet the Creator of everything sacrificed His Son to pay the penalty of our condemnation, so that we wouldn't have to, the sense of elitism fades in the face of God's amazing love and grace.

Visit **2xalt.com/meaning-of-life.html**
to learn more and to request a free copy of Scripture.

Martial Art of Performance

Join the Leadership Development Program designed to develop Leadership 2Xalt Performance™. Our programs are designed to provide Education, Application, and Integration.

EDUCATION	APPLICATION	INTEGRATION
Builds knowledge by providing facts, information, and basic skills	Builds understanding through the development of comprehension, insight, and sound judgment	Leads to wisdom through cultivating a culture of discernment and action
Seminars, Books, Articles, and other Study Materials	Courses and Workshops	Leadership Coaching

Become Certified in STAR Leadership through mastering the concepts of Strategic Leadership, Tactical Leadership, and Performance Leadership.

Green Belt	Brown Belt	Black Belt
Master the concepts of Strategic Leadership	Master the concepts of Tactical Leadership	Master the concepts of Performance Leadership

Contact 2Xalt today and get started on your certification!

2Xalt.com